The Changing Village Environment in Southeast Asia

The Changing Village Environment in Southeast Asia follows the work of the Good Roots Project, which is based on the island of Luzon in the northern Philippines. The Good Roots Project is a multi-year forestry and agriculture research project and an attempt on the part of industry, government, and science to better understand the processes of deforestation and initiate a strategy by which stressed upland ecosystems can be returned to productive stability.

The project examines the methods and results of five years of environmental research and development among the Ilocano and Yapayao speakers of northern Luzon. This comparative study of the lowland rural population and the upland minority population seeks to establish a multipurpose methodology which focuses on helping the farmers of the island to help themselves.

As director of the project, Ben J. Wallace analyzes the issues surrounding the project, how the initiatives have been implemented, and the future for the island as the population growth rate continues to rise and increasingly more land is given over to agriculture.

Ben J. Wallace is Professor of Anthropology, Assistant Provost and Director of Study Abroad Programs at Southern Methodist University, USA.

The Modern Anthropology of Southeast Asia Series
Edited by Victor T. King
University of Hull

William D. Wilder
University of Durham

The books in this series incorporate basic ethnographic description into a wider context of responses to development, globalisation and change. Each book embraces broadly the same concerns, but the emphasis in each differs as authors choose to concentrate on specific dimensions of change or work out particular conceptual approaches to the issues of development. Areas of concern include: nation-building, technological innovations in agriculture, rural–urban migration, the expansion of industrial and commercial employment, the rapid increase in cultural and ethnic tourism, the consequences of deforestation and environmental degradation, the 'modernisation of tradition', ethnic identity and conflict, and the religious transformation of society.

The Modern Anthropology of Southeast Asia
An introduction
Victor T. King and William D. Wilder

The Changing Village Environment in Southeast Asia
Applied anthropology and environmental reclamation
in the northern Philippines
Ben J. Wallace

The Changing World of Bali
Religion, society and tourism
Leo Howe

The Changing Village Environment in Southeast Asia

Applied anthropology and environmental reclamation in the northern Philippines

Ben J. Wallace

Routledge
Taylor & Francis Group

LONDON AND NEW YORK

First published 2006
by Routledge
2 Park Square, Milton Park, Abingdon, Oxon OX14 4RN

Simultaneously published in the USA and Canada
by Routledge
270 Madison Ave, New York, NY 10016

Routledge is an imprint of the Taylor & Francis Group

© 2006 Ben J. Wallace

Typeset in Sabon by
Newgen Imaging Systems (P) Ltd, Chennai, India
Printed and bound in Great Britain by
TJ International Ltd, Padstow, Cornwall

British Library Cataloguing in Publication Data
A catalogue record for this book is available from the
British Library

Library of Congress Cataloging in Publication Data
A catalog record for this book has been requested

ISBN 0–415–36484–1

Contents

Illustrations

Plates

Figures

Map

Tables

Preface

More than three decades ago, while sitting in a mountain forest on Northern Luzon, an old woman told me in her own language: "*Pekatoletam yo mula a ya'da na lubag ana yo lubag akanen detam.*" This roughly translates into English as "We eat the plants that the earth gives us and the earth eats us." This old woman, uneducated and a member of a tribal minority, impressed me so much with her ecological insight that this thought has stayed with me for all these years. Her understanding of human–nature relationships is a constant reminder that humanity and nature are interdependent parts of the whole. Humankind takes from nature and, in return, nature takes from humanity. In a harmonious world, there would be a balance in nature such that the human populations, and flora and fauna populations, would exist and die according to the laws of nature. Unfortunately, over the past hundred years, the equilibrium between humanity and nature has been dramatically disrupted through the acts of man— through deforestation. Humankind has taken too much from nature.

The Good Roots Project of Northern Luzon (focusing here on the years 1992–1996) is an attempt on the part of industry, government, and science to help humanity return to nature some of that which has been taken from her. It is unrealistic to believe that nature can be returned to its pristine state, but it is possible to stop the rate of destruction of the forests of the Philippines and to stabilize the rural environment. This is what Good Roots is about: helping farmers to help themselves to reclaim their environment.

It had been my good fortune to have the opportunity to assume the challenge of designing and directing the Good Roots Project. Importantly, however, Good Roots is an environmental project of and for hundreds of concerned people. Numerous individuals from science, government, and industry have contributed ideas and worked on the project as well.

Ever since an autumn day in late 1990, when Raymond F. Johnson, then Chairman and CEO of Caltex Petroleum, encouraged me to pursue the dream of a long-term research and development project in the Philippines, numerous people have contributed to the Good Roots Project.

Without the generous financial support of Caltex (Philippines) Inc. (now a member of the ChevronTexaco organization), Good Roots could not have operated. I am profoundly grateful for this support. My *utang na loob* ("debt of the heart"), however, is reserved for the employees (especially Marian Catedral, Rachel Alzona, and Cherry Ramos) of this Philippine institution who have provided logistical support and encouragement to Good Roots for many years.

Numerous individuals from the Philippine Department of Environment and Natural Resources (DENR), partners in the Good Roots Project deserve special acknowledgment for their contributions. First, I want to extend my gratitude to the Honorable Angel Alcala, an outstanding scientist and Secretary of DENR during the early years of Good Roots, for his interest and support. I also own a debt of gratitude to Drs Carlos Tomboc and Florendo Barangan of the DENR for their help and encouragement.

From my own institution, Southern Methodist University in Dallas, I am indebted to many individuals for insuring that my duties at SMU allowed me to reside several months each year in the Philippines.

The heart of any interdisciplinary research and development project is the scientific and support staff. In my view, the staff of the Good Roots Project is simply the best. I will remain always indebted to the initial Good Roots staff: Marilyn U. Tolentino (social sciences and Officer in Charge (OIC)), Gemma Domile (extension), Antonio Garvida (agriculture and forestry), Manuelito Calventas (agriculture and forestry), Magel Leaño (office manager) for their untiring work, dedication, insight and friendship through the early years of Good Roots. I also want to express my deep appreciation to Ann S. Wallace who freely gave of her time and insight, particularly in photographic and video documentation of the project.

If the heart of Good Roots is the scientific and support staff, then the soul of Good Roots is comprised of the farming men and women of the communities in Ilocos Norte. The successes of Good Roots are a tribute to their willingness to learn, teach, work, and take control of their destiny so that their children might have an opportunity to mature into Filipino citizens living in a greener, healthier and more productive environment.

To those who have contributed to Good Roots, I extend my heartfelt gratitude and I wish to all a personal *ugat ng buhay*.

Finally, for their assistance in helping me turn the work of the Good Roots Project into a monograph for *The Modern Anthropology of Southeast Asia Serie*s, I want to express my sincere appreciation to the series editors, Victor T. King and William D. Wilder.

Ben J. Wallace
Pugo, La Union
2005

Abbreviations

DENR   Department of Environment and Natural Resources
FAO   Food and Agriculture Organization
FSR/D   Farming Systems Research and Development
IFI   *Iglesia Filipina Independiente*
MPRT   Multipurpose Research Team
MPTS   Multipurpose tree species
NASA   National Aeronautics and Space Administration
NPA   National People's Army
OIC   Officer in Charge
RRA   Rapid Rural Appraisal

1 The Good Roots Project

Introduction

Maximo Bugay and his wife Maria worry that when the rainy season comes their house will be washed away by a mudslide. The Bugays do not live near an active volcano where, everyday, the residents suffer from an act of nature. Instead, their modest thatched house is located in a remote region more than 300 kilometers north of Mt Pinatubo, an active volcano in Philippines. They, like the people near Mt Pinatubo, however, worry about mudslides, but their fear does not come because of an act of nature; theirs is the direct result of an act of human intervention into nature. Maximo, Maria, and their neighbors have cut the trees from the mountain slopes above their village and know that it is only a matter of time—a week or a year before the erosion patterns are transformed into disastrous mudslides. For years, the farmers in this area chose not to acknowledge that they were living below an imminent tragedy. Now they take the situation seriously, and at a village meeting agreed to a ban on farming and tree-cutting above the village. Although this responsible act could save the houses of the Bugays and their neighbors, it may mark the beginning of a similar catastrophe for a nearby village; the Bugays and their friends are now cutting trees for fuelwood above this neighboring village.

This act of human intervention into nature is the primary stimulant creating the potential tragedy for the Bugay family and their neighbors. The situation has become the norm rather than the exception in upland areas throughout the tropical world. It is more than environmental or academic rhetoric to note that the planet Earth loses millions of hectares of critically valuable forests each year, much of which is brought about by human interaction with nature (cf. Barraclough and Ghimire 2000; Brown and Pearce 1994; FAO 2001, 2003a,b; Miller and Tangley 1991; Myers 1980; Nadkarni 1989; Sponsel *et al.* 1996;

Withington *et al.* 1988). Figures differ, but in Southeast Asia, somewhere between 40 and 60 percent of tropical and subtropical forest has been depleted over the past 100 years. Food and Agriculture Organization (FAO), in its *State of the World's Forest 2001*, reports that between 1990 and 2000, Southeast Asia lost forest cover five times faster than the rest of the world. Indonesia, Myanmar, Malaysia, and Thailand had the highest loss rate during this period, losing more than 100,000 hectares of forest annually. Based on studies of satellite imagery by National Aeronautics and Space Administration (NASA), the world's rainforests will vanish within the next 100 years (NASA 1998). FAO, in its *State of the World's Forest 2003*, reports that 0.38 percent of the world's forests were converted to other land uses during the 1990s.

In the Philippines, forests covered more than 20 million hectares a hundred years ago, or about 70 percent of the total land area (Wernstedt and Spencer 1967). By 1970, Philippine forestland had declined to approximately 10 million hectares, and by 1990, it had dropped to 6 million hectares (Uitamo 1999). Although around 70 percent of the land in the Philippines was covered with forest in the past, only 20 percent of the land is now covered with forest. This is an alarming situation that is only going to worsen as the population growth rates continue to rise and increasingly more land is given over to agriculture.

Whereas it is true that in the Philippines and other Southeast Asian nations it is human intervention into nature, through the uses and misuses of technological practices and perceptions, which primarily account for deforestation, such an observation is a dramatic oversimplification of the situation. In some cases, as in illegal logging, for example, some of the villagers show a complete disregard for the effects of their destructive activity. In other situations, such as securing fuelwood, the farmers have little or no choice but to cut trees from the forest as alternative fuel sources are either unavailable or are too expensive. In the case of slash-and-burn or shifting cultivation, while primary forest may be destroyed, if practiced in 4–5 year cycles in secondary forest, a stable population can exist for several decades without bringing about further destruction to the ecosystem. Fundamentally, whether shifting cultivation, household construction, or illegal logging, each mechanism of human intervention into nature needs to be examined within its immediate cultural and environmental context.

In an attempt to better understand the processes of deforestation and initiate a strategy by which stressed upland ecosystems can be returned to productive stability, a multi-year forestry and agriculture research project is underway in the Philippines. This research and development project was initiated in 1991 in far Northern Luzon, moved to southern Luzon in 1996, and now operates in central Luzon.

Good Roots

Since the Second World War and the emergence of new nation states, particularly in Africa and Asia, the primary burden for funding and carrying out the economic development of these Third World nations has fallen to the governments using local funds, as well as grants, contracts, and loans from donor agencies such as the World Bank, Asian Development Bank, and the major developmental arms of industrial nations such as the United States, France, Japan, and Germany (Rutten 1982). Industry, the group most criticized for destroying the environment is prominently absent from a list of donor agencies putting their resources and talents to work to solve the problems of rural development. Action has been taken in the Philippines to rectify this situation.

A memorandum of agreement on agroforestry research and development was signed on Earth Day, 1991, between Southern Methodist University (Institute for the Study of Earth and Man), Caltex (Philippines) Inc., and the Philippine Department of Environment and Natural Resources (DENR). This research and development project is a pioneer action in the Philippines because it is the first example of industry, government and the academic community pooling their resources and talents, and directing them toward the amelioration of some of the environmental and social problems facing this predominantly rural country. The initiator and overall director of the project, an anthropologist from Southern Methodist University, is responsible for overseeing all the scientific and developmental activity and holds final authority in this arena. Caltex Philippines provides the funds for the project and has final responsibility on a pre-approved budget. Finally, the Philippine DENR monitors the scientific activities of the project, provides technical advice, and liaises with other government agencies. This project, technically entitled "Multipurpose Tree Species, Wood Use and Farming Systems Research," is popularly known simply as "Good Roots—*Ugat ng buhay*."

A major concern of Good Roots has been to develop the case for interdisciplinary research and development where in order to maximize the accomplishments of team members and minimize costs, all parts of the project are perceived of as functionally interrelated such that any component or activity (e.g. personnel, land, research activity, etc.) is multipurpose. Just as a multipurpose tree (Von Carlowitz 1984) is a tree that contributes in more than one way to the sustainability of an agro-forestry system, multipurpose research, as used here, is research in which each activity contributes in more than one way to the sustain-ability and the attainment of the goals of the project. Research team members, constituting what may be called a Multipurpose Research Team (MPRT), function as partially interchangeable parts of the whole and contribute in more than one way to the sustainability of research and development activities. Illustrative materials here are drawn from the Good Roots Project as carried out in the province of Ilocos Norte, Philippines between the years 1992 and 1997 (see Wallace 1995b, 2001). Good Roots in Ilocos Norte was turned over to the local farmers in 1996 and is still benefiting the families of the area.

A major feature of Good Roots is to facilitate research and develop-ment on multipurpose tree species (MPTS) (i.e. tree species that perform more than a single biological or social function) within the context of the whole farm or farming system. Good Roots is not a forestry project where hundreds of hectares of denuded hill slopes are reclaimed through the planting of selected tree species. Large-scale reforestation projects such as these are best left to large government agencies where hundreds of laborers can be employed to plant seedlings. The Good Roots Project is carried out in four communities located in the most northwestern province of the Philippines. Good Roots is a sustainable and integrated agroforestry research and development project devoted to helping farm families improve their farms and reclaim the areas surrounding their farms by promoting native species and integrating species proven suc-cessful elsewhere such that stressed environments may be stabilized and the quality of life for farming men, women, and children of the area is improved.

The Good Roots communities

The agroforestry activities of Good Roots are carried out in and around four villages located along the western foothills of the Cordillera Central in the northern most municipality in the Philippine province of Ilocos Norte. San Isidro, Dampig, and Subec (with populations of 663, 773, and 1,142 respectively; see Table 1.1) are representative of many low-land Ilocano communities or *barangay*. In the Philippines, a politically defined municipal entity—similar to a town—consists of one or more *barangay*. The fourth village, Saliksik, has a population of 176 people, all of whom are members of the ethnic minority Apayao-Isneg, known locally as Yapayao. There are 196 households in Subec, 134 households in Dampig, 108 households in San Isidro, and 35 households in Saliksik.

Table 1.1 Good Roots *barangay*

Barangay	Population	Households
Dampig	773	134
Subec	1,142	196
San Isidro	663	108
Saliksik	176	35

Excluding the residents of the nearby *poblacion*, the immediate villages around the Good Roots communities number six *barangay* and have a total population of 5,246, that is, the Good Roots communities represent 34 percent of the total *barangay* population of the immediate area. The nearest town, Pagudpud, has a *poblacion* population of 4,059 people. The total population of the municipality of Pagudpud, in landmass one of the largest in Ilocos Norte, is 17,417. The houses in the project are situated in elevations ranging from 15 meters above sea level (the lowest house in Subec) to 415 meters (the highest makeshift house in Saliksik).

Pagudpud is located 89 kilometers north of the provincial capital of Laoag.

Ilocano, regardless of their present location, usually claim the provinces of Ilocos Norte and Ilocos Sur as their homeland. Informants often are quick to point out that the Ilocano are very hard workers because the environment of these provinces is so harsh. In fact, this narrow strip of flatland, bordered on the East by the Cordillera Central and on the West by the South China Sea is limited in natural resources. Most of the primary forest has been destroyed. Intensive tobacco cultivation since the days of the Spanish has weakened the productivity of much of the land, and, the area is marked by a distinct wet and dry season with 5–6 months of the year being dry (cf. Jocano 1982; Werndstedt and Spencer 1967).

The people of these communities were selected for study and development because their agricultural technologies and the environmental zones in which they live are representative of the western coastal plane of northern Luzon (Map 1.1). The agricultural technology of San Isidro is predominantly one of irrigated paddy rice cultivation, with lesser amount of rainfed plow farming (Figure 1.1). Dampig is both a rainfed and an irrigated paddy farming community. The people of Subec have a farming technology of both irrigated paddy rice and dry field cultivation. The people of Saliksik primarily practice slash-and-burn or swidden cultivation. "*Kaingin*" is the term applied

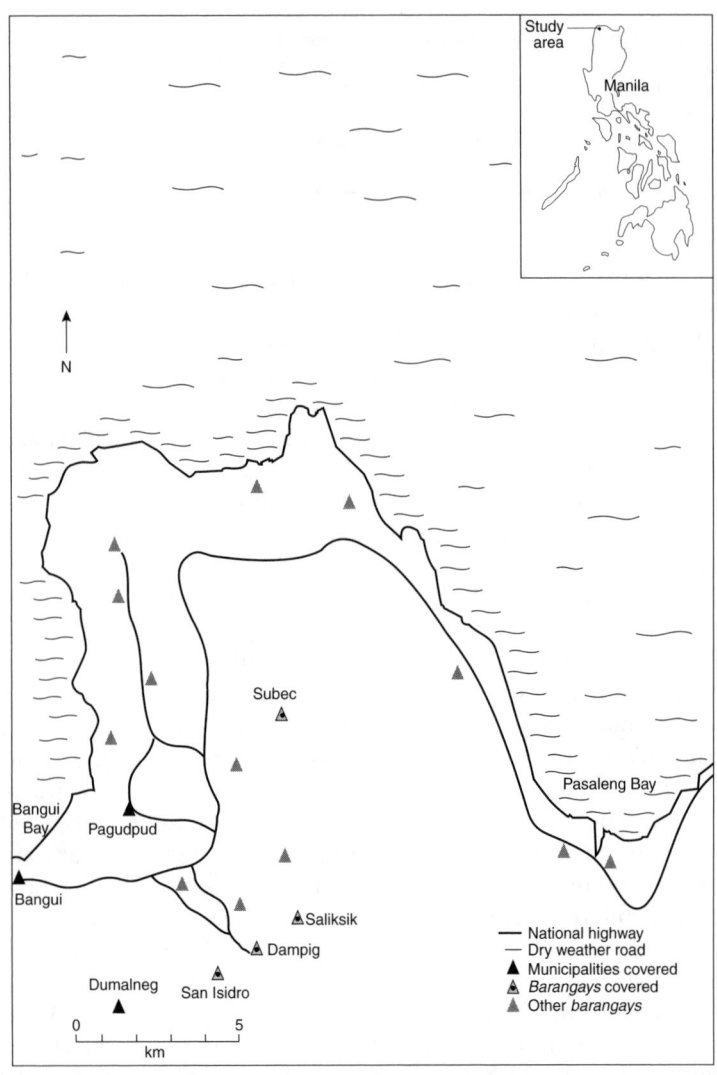

Map 1.1 Map of Northern Luzon and Pagudpud.

to most forms of upland cultivation in the Philippines. Some minor *kaingin* activity also can be found in all three of the Ilocano communities. Although these four villages are situated only 4–8 kilometers from the South China Sea, the villagers perceive of themselves as

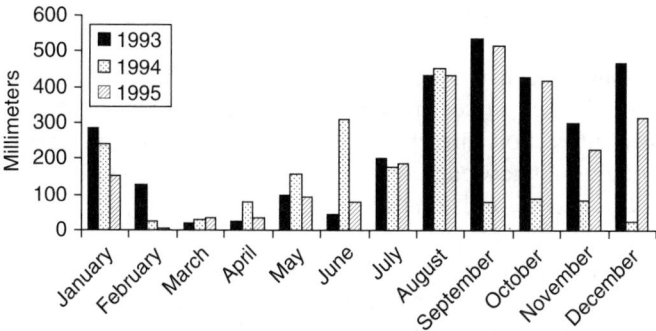

Figure 1.1 Rainfall: Pagudpud.

agriculturalists, the Ilocano identifying with the lowlands and the Yapayao identifying with the mountains.

The multipurpose research experience

In the field of community development, especially in agriculture and agroforestry research, the trend over the past few decades has been toward an interdisciplinary orientation. Although it is clear that under certain circumstances interdisciplinary research is an improvement over a discipline-based approach, interdisciplinary research has not met with complete success. There is nothing inherently incompatible between, for example, a forester conducting experiments on the nitrogen-fixing capabilities of *Leucaena* spp. and an anthropologist determining the folk taxonomy of a people's species preferences for fuelwood. In reality, however, the two researchers bring to their activity a different set of disciplinary biases and are often in their view, attempting to solve unrelated issues. Synthesis, almost by definition, under these conditions becomes a seemingly impossible task. As a consequence, interdisciplinary research and development are more often than not, multidisciplinary research and development masked behind the facade of the more trendy concept of "interdisciplinary" research (Wallace 1991). Even in cases which claim an interdisciplinary team of specialists—perhaps an economist, an anthropologist and an agriculturist—because of disciplinary biases, there is a tendency for the researchers to work independently and later come together and attempt to integrate the data so that a workable policy can be implemented. About one of the most successful models for rural development, Farming Systems Research and Development (FSR/D), where interdisciplinary is a key concept, Shaner *et al.* (1982: 185) say:

> Although much is written about interdisciplinary and its definitions, the key ingredient for true interdisciplinary is *interaction*. This interaction invariably leads to synthesis and synergism. Synthesis of knowledge among interacting disciplines produces new ideas, concept, and solutions.

Although as part of a model, this is an accurate statement of an ideal, even in cases that have met with considerable success, such as at the International Potato Center discussed by Rhoades *et al.* (1986), disciplinary biases often limit success. As these researchers have noted (1986: 38):

> It is our hunch that most successful teams experience rough going. This to a great degree grows from the difficult nature of on-farm research activities. Combining disciplines, executing on-farm experiments, functioning under the sometimes ludicrous conditions of underdeveloped regions, reconciling personality differences, writing joint papers, etc. are all difficult tasks which can be disastrous. This, as we have noted, is what drives teams often to the "multidisciplinary" approach, wherein team members pursue disciplinary research and pass back and forth jargon-ridden, mutually incomprehensible reports. It is passed as interdisciplinary research and it satisfies donors, but it is not the real thing.

One way to reduce conflicts arising from disciplinary biases, enhance interaction, improve productivity, reduce costs, and generally improve research and development effectiveness is to structure the project so that as many components as possible of the undertaking serve multipurpose functions.

It became clear early in the negotiations with industry to fund the Good Roots Project that it would be necessary to respond to the reasonable expectations that the proposed project be able to show results in a relatively short period of time, that the project be cost-effective, and that it not be burdened with the kind of costly bureaucracy (buildings, secretaries, consultants, research stations, vehicles, etc.) so often associated with agriculture and agroforestry development projects. The problem, simply stated, became: how to do quality agroforestry research and development, benefiting a relatively large number of people, at a fraction of the cost often spent by international donor agencies. This meant that instead of spending 5, 8, 20, or even 40 million dollars over five years, common practice by international standards, the budget would be limited to approximately $1\frac{1}{2}$ million dollars over five years. This meant that instead of 20, 40 or even more employees, there could be only 4–6, there could be no office building, research stations would be too costly, instead of numerous trucks there could be only one, and expatriate consultants would have to be severely limited. The challenge became how to control costs and create an MPRT to address the demands of multipurpose research and development within a FSR/D approach (CGIAR 1978; De Walt 1985; Jones and Wallace 1986; Norman *et al.* 1979; Rhoades 1985; Shaner *et al.* 1982), especially as related to FSR/D and MPTS (Wallace 1989).

Because Good Roots was to be carried out within the context of FSR, it was important to take into consideration a major criticism of FSR/D; namely, that the project not fall into the trap of too narrowly operationalizing the approach into a biotechnical activity. As succinctly noted by Raintree and Hoskins (1988: 39):

> One inadequacy of such an approach is immediately obvious to anyone familiar with the existing institutionalization of FSR. With a few rare exceptions, research is almost never thought of as referring to anything outside a very narrow brand of biotechnical experimentation. The socioeconomic dimensions of technology development may be taken up, but usually only in a service capacity and not as a proper research subject in their own right, and the organizational aspects of extension are almost never considered at all within the formal research structures. These are thought of, if they are thought of at all, simply as externalities over which the researcher has no control, and no legitimate institutional interest.

Or as noted by the forester Raros (1987: 71):

> The task calls for a reorientation of manpower education training. It demands more than substantive integration of knowledge and skills in technical agriculture and forestry; it obliges the social sciences to play the more aggressive, if not leading, rather than simply supportive role.

These cautions were integrated into the Good Roots design to insure that the old biotechnical and top-down approaches to agriculture and forestry development were avoided. Fundamentally, the MPTS-based farming systems approach adopted by Good Roots involves the study and development of a land-use strategy maximizing the interrelated production of forestry, agricultural, and animal products. This encompasses the social, cultural, and political factors conditioning these variables, and a wide array of methods, ranging from participant observation to Rapid Rural Appraisal (RRA) (Khon Kaen University 1987) and questionnaires, are employed. To accomplish this goal, the program has adopted the following three-stage procedure as the foundation of its MPTS–FSR approach (Jones and Wallace 1986):

1   Identification of the tree components in the area and the farmer's perception and use of trees in the farming system.
2   On farm trials of MPTS which are perceived by both farmers and researchers to be of value.
3   Establish a relationship between researchers and farmers such that they enter into a collaborative relationship promoting the use of MPTS.

The goals of the Good Roots Project are accomplished through the efforts of an MPRT which is composed of five people: a male anthropologist, a male agriculturist, a male forester, a female social science specialist, and a female extension specialist. An adequate MPRT in the Philippines, as well as in many other parts of the world, should include both male and female researchers. Farming activity and related cultural beliefs are often gender specific and are most efficiently addressed in like-gender situations. But, even when the various farming tasks are conducted by both males and females, a mixed-gender team is the most effective because an interdisciplinary approach to farming involves an examination of farm families and all farmers: men, women, and children.

An expensive part of most international development projects is the costs of permanent scientific personnel and local and expatriate consultants. Good Roots Project costs are reduced by employing a small scientific staff and keeping the only expatriate member of the team, the initiator and director, in the field for only 3 or 4 months a year. Local and expatriate consultants do not have to be hired because "expert" advice is provided by the Philippine DENR, co-participants in the project.

The other team members are Filipinos with considerable experience in research and development. Considering that the director of the project is an anthropologist with more than three decades of research and development experience in Southeast Asia, while designing the Good Roots research and development activity, it was decided that the goals of the project could best be attained, with a team consisting of a forester, an agriculturist, a social science specialist, and an extension specialist. Time has shown that this is a very good mix of personnel for a project like Good Roots. In interviewing potential researchers, it was important to identify individuals who not only were competent but who were self-confident enough not to be threatened in a team situation and who had enough experience to recognize the limitations of a "bureaucratic mentality." Because Ilocano is the *lingua franca* of the region, it was further decided that these researchers ideally should be native Ilocano speakers and from the general region of the area where the project was to be conducted. Selecting researchers who already had some familiarity with the research area greatly reduced the adjustment-time in the field situation.

In order to secure the services of the best available Filipino scientific personnel and because the duties are demanding, the researchers are paid approximately 30 percent more than they would receive in comparable positions in government service. Although each team member brings a particular specialty to the project and has primary responsibility in his or her arena, the member's actual responsibilities involve much more. Although the personnel are not interchangeable parts of the whole, they function effectively in roles in which they were not originally trained. Each team member has trained his or her colleagues in the fundamentals of his or her discipline such that the social scientist, for example, can function with minimal help in some agricultural research or the forester can function effectively in some social science research. The agriculturist has not been fully trained as a social scientist but he has learned sufficient skills in social science research to carry out specific research tasks or serve as an assistant on a particular task. The same is also true of the other researchers on the team. For example, when the forester is not propagating plants or establishing plant nurseries, he may be assisting the social scientist in conducting socio-economic surveys or interviewing farmers on the social aspects of farming. When the social scientist is not interviewing farmer participants, she may be assisting the agriculturist in drawing up or compiling an inventory of the usable plant species in the area. If the extension specialist is not busy assisting farmers in organizing themselves into work groups, she may be tabulating economic and botanical data. Drawing from a carefully structured but flexible research design, decisions in research and development implementation are made by consensus with the appropriately trained scientist providing guidance. In Good Roots, the team is the responsible unit—not individuals. Relying on an MPRT eliminates downtime, redundancy, and builds *esprit de corps* leading to productivity. Personnel from the Philippine DENR also are involved in monitoring the activities of the flexible research design.

The multipurpose character of the research team also applies to support personnel: a secretary/accountant, a utility person/driver, and even the cook. All personnel, including these, were informed when they were hired that in addition to their primary duties, they, for example, would also be expected to work in the plant nurseries, assist the research team in counting trees, or do something as simple as watering the seedlings.

The multipurpose concept along with and other cost-saving measures have been applied to numerous aspects of the Good Roots Project. First, the project has no office building or suite of offices. Instead, it is operated out of a modest rented house in the field that serves as an office and also as living quarters for all project personnel. Not only does this reduce costs, living and working together creates a situation conducive to teamwork and a mechanism by which productive time is maximized. For example, the team generally works 10–12 hours a day and occasionally, seven days a week depending on the needs of the farmer participants. Because Good Roots activity is farmer-intensive, research team members have to adjust their agenda to fit the agricultural cycle of the region and the time the farmers have to devote to the project. From the perspective of interdisciplinary research and development, living and working together clearly promotes the all-important ingredient of interaction. Family life occasionally suffers from this kind of dedication to the project but since all team members are aware of the potential for "neglect," considerable effort is devoted to insuring that each team member is able to spend quality time with his or her family. In general, based on the Good Roots experience, the benefits of the team working and living together in the same facility greatly overshadow any problems. An added benefit to this aspect of the multipurpose approach is the savings in overhead expenses. The overhead expenses for Good Roots, around 7 percent of the total budget, is significantly lower than many international donor projects which, in some cases, permit up to 25 percent of the budget for overhead activity.

Nursery costs also have been minimized. Good Roots nurseries, one surrounding the office/dwelling of the research team and 1 or 2 in each of the 4 research villages, are located on plots of land that were previously not used for productive farming activity. In the case of the nursery at the office/dwelling, the land is a yard area. In the case of the four research villages, the communities provide space for the nurseries as a part of their contribution to Good Roots. With guidance from the research team, the farm families in the four communities have organized themselves into the Good Roots Agroforestry Association with elected officials and have established 1 or 2 nurseries in each community. The Good Roots participants work closely with the research team in propagating seeds, tending seedlings, and planning a strategy for integrating the seedlings into the agroforestry system. The nurseries are located in the research and development communities so as to maximize the benefits to the local farm families. In the case of the nursery among the Yapayao, located two hours away—on foot from the nearest dry season road, but as in the case of all Good Roots nurseries, it is placed for the usefulness and education of the farmers, not for the convenience of the research team or to show visiting dignitaries. The nurseries themselves are multipurpose. They not only fulfill their primary function of a place for seedling development, but they also serve as a meeting place for Good Roots Agroforestry Association meetings, a relaxed gathering point for participants to visit and "gossip" while tending to the seedlings, and they provide a reference group point of identity for many of the villagers. Importantly, the benefits from the nurseries and the Good Roots Agroforestry Association come about at little or no financial cost to the project.

Financial expenditures have been reduced further by eliminating research stations and associated fields from the project. The research station of Good Roots is the land of the farmers. All crop and MPTS trials are carried out on and around the existing lands of Good Roots participants. For example, Good Roots maintains a demonstration plot where various species trials and farming techniques are showcased. The land for the demonstration plot is provided by a participant farm family and labor is the responsibility of local farmers. An exception to this generalization is a Good Roots fuelwood tree farm that has been established with the cooperation of the Philippine DENR, on public lands.

As a result of the Good Roots experience, the multipurpose nature of farmland in the area is expanded because of the farm families' willingness to devote some of it to nurseries, demonstration plots, and experimental trials. Not only do their lands fulfill the primary function of providing fundamental subsistence for the farmers, they also serve the goals of Good Roots and contribute to the environmental stability of the region.

A final cost-saving measure contributing to the effectiveness of Good Roots is in compensation provided to the farm family participants for their labor and time. Unlike some development projects, especially forestry projects, Good Roots participants do not receive money for working in the nurseries or for planting trees. This is antithetical to the multipurpose foundation on which the project is based. Good Roots was never intended to be nor has it become a "plant for pay" project. The Good Roots farmers are full participants and an integral part of all development activity. It is the Good Roots farm families who are improving their farming system and reclaiming their environment; they are the beneficiaries of their own labors. This is sufficient payment. There are more farm families who want to participate in the program than can be accommodated by the research staff. In their efforts to stabilize their agroforestry system by working in the nurseries, integrating tree species into their farming system, and by generally participating in the Good Roots Agroforestry Association, the farmers are contributing to their own destiny. The primary function of the research team is to conduct research, provide guidance to the farmers, and create a camaraderie among the farmers so that enthusiasm for the project is maintained.

In terms of methodology and organization, the Good Roots Project draws heavily from the fields of traditional field ethnography, FSRD, and RRA. From the perspective of field ethnography, the researchers perceive their work as relatively long-term, and view a society as consisting of interrelated biological, cultural, social, and political components, they live in the field, speak the local language, and rely heavily on participant observation as an information-gathering tool. From the perspective of FSR/D, the research team is interdisciplinary, farming is defined as a system encompassing the spatial and temporal juxtapositions of crops, trees, farm animals and humans, research involves the identification of problems and systems, baseline surveys, on-farm experiments, the design of improved systems, and the validation, recommendation, and evaluation of technologies. From RRA, Good Roots has taken a flexible methodology, a small team approach, a reliance on key informants as well as group interviews, scheduled interaction for team members, and team discussion and analysis of integrated quantifiable and non-quantifiable data. In Good Roots, a MPRT follows a multipurpose methodology to bring about multipurpose research and development.

The Good Roots multipurpose model may not be suitable for all research and development projects in agroforestry but it is an interdisciplinary model that has proven to be successful in one region of the northern Philippines. Farmers and researchers are cooperating to bring stability to a region under environmental degradation—to reestablish a balance between people and nature within a reasonable timeframe, and at a reasonable cost. Scholars and researchers may disagree on the exact approach to be followed but many will agree that it will take an interdisciplinary-research effort to address the environmental problems characterizing all regions of the world. The Good Roots experience suggests that in certain situations, the disciplinary constraints retarding the potential of interdisciplinary research and development may be corrected by adopting a multipurpose research and development model.

2 The Ilocano

Introduction

After the Spanish conquistadors took control of the Manila area, they turned their attention to dominating other parts of the Philippines. One such expedition, captained by Juan de Salcedo, the 22-year-old grandson of Miguel Lopez de Legaspi, generally considered the conqueror of the Philippines, sailed up the west coast of Luzon in 1572 in search of reported gold mines, which had been exploited in earlier centuries by the Japanese and Chinese. As the ships neared the most northern areas of Luzon, they could see that the coastline was dotted with sheltered coves or bays, in Tagalog called "*looc.*" Consequently, the Spanish named the region "*Ylocos,*" and the local people, "*Ylocanos.*"

Many Ilocano resisted the abusive and dictatorial actions of the Augustinian friars, but the revolts were generally unsuccessful. Two of the early and most noteworthy Ilocano resistance fighters were Diego Silang and his wife, Gabriela. Diego Silang led a series of battles against the Spanish in 1762, only to be killed by an assassin. His wife, Gabriela, took up his cause. She was captured and hanged. This man and wife are considered two of the first of a long line of Filipino resistance fighters who died at the hands of the Spanish. Other Ilocano uprisings against the Spanish met with a similar fate.

Because of rapid population growth, general political unrest, and in an attempt by the Spanish to better control the area, in 1818, Ilocos was divided by Royal decree into two provinces, Ilocos Norte and Ilocos Sur.

Rural Ilocanos in the Pagudpud area believe themselves to be honest, industrious, hardworking, and long-suffering because of what they perceive as a difficult environment in which to live. This perception of a "hard life," mixed with limited natural resources, and a high population density by the middle of the nineteenth century (Smith 1981) served as stimuli prompting the Ilocano to become the most migratory of Philippine populations. Ilocano has become the lingua franca of most of Luzon north of Manila. The Ilocano pioneered colonization throughout the southern islands of the Philippines, and constitute the majority of US Filipino-Americans.

The Ilocano communities of San Isidro, Dampig, and Subec

The Good Roots communities of San Isidro (108 households), Dampig (134 households), and Subec (196 households) are representative of other rural Ilocano communities in the municipality of Pagudpud, Ilocos Norte, and elsewhere on Northern Luzon (cf. Benner 2001; Jocano 1982; Lee 1985; Lewis 1971, 1991). There are a few financially secure families in these three communities, due mainly to monetary repatriation from relatives working abroad, but the majority of the families are small land owners of less than a hectare, and they derive their living by farming and from small-time supplementary economic activities. The residents of the area often claim with pride that they are the "pure" Ilocanos, their isolation serving as a barrier from being dominated by the Spanish. Ilocanos from other parts of Ilocos Norte and Ilocos Sur also make this claim.

When the Good Roots Project started, the paved national highway from the south ended in Pagudpud. A few years later, the last 22 kilometers of dirt and occasionally impassable road was paved, thus linking the western and eastern sides of the Cordillera Central by public bus traffic. This exposed Pugudpud to considerably more commercial influence. The roads from the *poblacion* to San Isidro, Dampig, and Subec are dirt, and during the rainy season, are occasionally impassable to jeepney or tricycle traffic.

The municipality of Pagudpud, like other municipalities in the country, is governed by an elected mayor, a vice mayor, and a municipal council consisting of eight elected persons. The smallest political unit is the *purok* or neighborhood. Several *purok* constitute a *barangay*, and several *barangay*, depending on the population of the area, comprise the municipality. Each *barangay* is headed by an elected *barangay* captain, assisted by elected councilors.

Although the *purok* is the smallest political unit of the community, its leaders have considerable "power" in matters of the daily operation of the neighborhood. Minor theft, arguments between families, drunkenness, control of stray animals, and even adultery fall under the purview of the *purok* leader and his or her council. The goal is to deal as much as possible with local social problems at the *purok* level of community organization. Disruptive social problems that cannot be solved by *purok* officials are brought to the attention of the *barangay* captain and the *barangay* council. At the *purok* and *barangay* level, justice is based on common sense and rural etiquette guided by Philippine law. Issues that are more serious such as murder or major theft is dealt with by the municipal and provincial authorities.

Although most observers of Philippine politics would agree that elections are usually heated, often nasty, and sometime deadly, Pagudpud is consider even more of a "hot spot." The primary reason for this is the competition between two rich and powerful families who have dominated Pagudpud and the adjacent municipality for over thirty years. In this frontier area, with roads to be built, with outstanding tourist potential, and land available for annexation, the financial stakes are high.

The son of the mayor from the adjacent town moved into Pagudpud. He ran for mayor and unseated the Pagudpud mayor of more than twenty-five years. The claim was that the new mayor paid ten times more for a vote than that the old mayor paid. The situation became so volatile that it erupted into a gun battle between the new mayor and the former mayor, and their bodyguards. During the fight, the former mayor was killed. The winner of the gun battle was acquitted of all charge of assault by the court in the provincial capital of Laoag.

The three Good Roots *barangay* are typical of the Ilocos area. Each has a modest *barangay* hall, where the *barangay* council meets, a small building which is used for visiting Philippine health officials and other government officials, and a smattering of small house-front stores called *sari-sari* selling candy, snacks, sodas, cigarettes, and alcohol. San Isidro, Dampig, and Subec all have an elementary school. The nearest high school is in an adjacent municipality.

Houses in the Good Roots *barangay* are clustered into small neighborhood units, often occupied by extended family members, and usually located along the few existing roads. House construction is determined by family income, the poorer the family, the more modest the house. Poor families construct their houses, usually with a central room and a bedroom, and a cooking-hearth area, from bamboo. These houses usually have thatched roofs. The more substantial houses are made from milled lumber or from cinder blocks, and the roofs are usually of galvanized metal, so-called "tin roofs." These houses may have more than one bedroom, a living room, a kitchen area, and maybe even a veranda. Most houses have other structures such as pigpens, chicken coops, storage sheds, and a latrine near the main house.

Electricity, often interrupted with "brown-outs," is available in San Isidro, Dampig, and Subec, although not all families can afford the service. Water for the three communities comes from mountain springs.

Furnishings within the homes are directly related to the income of the family. Poor families have very little in the way of furnishings, often nothing more than a couple of home-made chairs and benches, a table, a few cooking utensils, and woven mats on which to sleep. Clothing is stored in trunks. The more economically secure families usually will have furnishing commensurate with their income; commercially made couches and chairs, window curtains, a radio, a television, fans, a small refrigerator, and an electric iron. The few wealthy families in the area purchased imported furnishings. Mainly, these wealthy families set themselves apart from community members with expensive automobiles, frequent trips abroad, and with bodyguards.

Farming

The basis of the economy of Subec, Dampig, and San Isidro is farming; mainly irrigated paddy rice cultivation and rain-fed dry field plow farming. The people of these communities are privileged because of a reasonably predictable water supply. Rivers and streams flowing down from the mountains have made it possible to develop an irrigation system in several parts of the area. The availability of water allows the farmers to cultivate some of the newer and faster, maturing varieties of rice. With these varieties, they can get two crops of rice per year. Where there is no irrigation, the farmers can get only one crop of rice per year. A few of the Ilocano families in these communities also practice slash-and-burn cultivation (*kaingin*), similar to that practice by the neighboring Yapayao (see Chapter 3), but it is economically insignificant.

For those farm families fortunate enough to own some irrigated land, the first rice cropping is May to October, and the second cropping is from November to March. In the areas where there is no irrigation, either in the uplands or lowlands, the farmers usually get only one rice crop a year. But, since Pagudpud often experiences strong northerly monsoon rainfall during November through January, which sometimes lasts into February, a few farm families occasionally risk a second rice planting. Most families, however, choose to plant cultigens such as pepper, eggplant, garlic, tomato, and other vegetables during the second season.

Traditionally among the Ilocano, planting rituals were observed, but today, such activity is considered a superstitious belief and not necessary to insure a bountiful crop. The fatalism of the Ilocano is reflected in his or her acceptance of *bahala na* or "what will be, will be." The success of crops depends primarily on rainfall patterns. As one

Ilocano said, "No rain, no farm." Occasionally, a devout Ilocano Catholic may have new agricultural equipment such as a motorized plow blessed or baptized by the local priest. A few of the older Ilocano men still adhere to the practice of placing a small bundle of the harvested *palay* (rice) in a hole near the corner of the field as an expression of gratitude for a good harvest. In general, however, farming for the Ilocano is a purely pragmatic and economic matter.

As noted, the Good Roots farm families in San Isidro, Dampig, and Subec do mainly either irrigated paddy rice farming or rain-fed dry field plow farming. Except for the fact that paddy rice is transplanted from seedling beds, the basic steps in paddy farming or dry field plow farming are very similar.

Farmers devote a significant amount of time to establishing and caring for their rice seedling beds. Usually in May (for the first planting season), farmers carefully plow and weed a small piece of land to serve as the seedling bed. The seeds are soaked and then sowed in June, and allowed to germinate. Careful attention is given to the application of fertilizer and the spraying of insecticides and pesticides. Great care must be taken in developing the seedling beds because if the seedlings do not mature healthy, the farmers will have little or no seedlings to transplant.

While the seedling beds mature, the farmer prepares his paddy for transplanting. The walls (*tombac*) of the paddy are repaired and weeds pulled. The farmer does the initial plowing of his paddy to coincide with the full maturation of the seedlings. The seedlings are uprooted, and then tied into bunches as preparation for transplanting.

As there are very few motorized paddy plows in the area, almost all plowing and harrowing is done with a water buffalo (*carabao*). If the farmer does not own a water buffalo, he will have to rent one from a neighbor, and hire someone to plow his paddy. The same applies to harrowing the field. In some cases, the cost for having a field plowed or to rent a water buffalo is paid directly, in other cases a small part of the crop paid out, and in others, labor reciprocity is the norm. Whatever the arrangement, plowing and harrowing is relatively fast and easy work for the farmer.

Planting rice is backbreaking work. A well-known Filipino children's song summarizes what all Filipino farmers know well.

> Planting rice is never fun.
> Bent from morn till the set of sun.
> Cannot stand and cannot sit.
> Cannot rest for a little bit.

The start of the transplanting activity in the Good Roots area is called in Ilocano "*tunek.*" Because of a need to regulate the flow of irrigation water, in some parts of Pagudpud, all transplanting is done within a day or two. Farmers who are late with their transplanting are fined an amount agreed upon the previous year by the local farmers' association. Where water does not have to be closely regulated, farmers can transplant at their convenience.

Transplanting a paddy field of around a 1,000 square meters in size will take 3–5 men or women less than a day. Men usually transplant, but occasionally women also work in this task. With fresh irrigation water standing in the paddy, bundles of seedlings are placed strategically around the paddy area. The planter then takes a bundle of seedlings, pulls a seedling from the bundle, and sticks its roots into the soil beneath the water. Some planters are so skilled that he or she can transplant a seedling in a matter of only 3–5 seconds.

Paddy rice cultivation

If there is to be a productive harvest, maintaining and protecting the paddy is critical (Table 2.1). Early in the growing season, one of the most critical problems the farmer has to face is the eradication of snails from the paddy. Care must be directed toward the application of fertilizers, and the use of pesticides. As the grain matures, birds become a problem. The farmer tries to frighten the birds with human-like scarecrows, as well as with ribbons and other objects that blow in the wind.

The water is drained from the field usually during late September and harvesting the grain (called *palay* at harvest) starts soon thereafter. If the paddy of the household is small, all members of the household over the age of about eleven years of age work in the harvest. If the farm is one-half or more of a hectare, the owner will usually have to hire day laborers to help in the harvest. In some cases, the laborer will be paid in cash. In other cases, the laborer may owe the owner of the farm money from a previous loan so he will repay the loan by working in the harvest. Finally, some of the laborers receive *palay* as payment for their labor. The crop is harvested by hand with a small hand-knife (*kumpay*), and tied into bundles for convenient storage and consumption.

After the harvest, the *palay* is dried under the heat of the sun for several days. Then, it is either stored or milled. If the family needs money, the *palay* may be immediately sold to rice-mill owners or other buyers.

Table 2.1 Paddy rice cultivation

Ilocano paddy activity	Month	Explanation
Panagaramid iti pagbunobonan	May	Preparing the seed bed, including weeding, harrowing, etc.
Panagbunobon	June	Sowing the seeds in the seed bed
Panangtaripato iti bunobon	June–July	Seedling care and maintenance
Panaggaikpanagparagus	June	Weeding the paddies and dikes
Panagarado	June	First plowing of the paddy
Panagmoriski	June–July	Harrowing
Panagkiwar	July	Final plowing
Panagtabtab	July	Final weeding and repairing paddy dikes
Panagraep	July	Transplanting
Panagabuno/panagdalus ti tambak	July–September	Crop maintenance and care of the paddy
Panagpadanum	July–September	Irrigating the rice
Panagbugaw	September	Protecting the crops from birds
Panagpaati	September	Draining the water from the fields
Panaggapas	October	Harvesting
Agirik/agasaksak	October	Threshing the grain
Panagbilag iti irik	October	Drying the *palay*
Panagidulin	October	Storing the *palay*
Panagpabayo	October	Milling the rice

Other sources of income and food

Almost all of the Ilocano families in the Good Roots *barangay* raise domestic animals; chickens, ducks, turkeys, pigeons, pigs, cattle, and water buffalo. The fowl are for home consumption, and are seldom sold. Pigs, cows, and *carabao* are considered economic assets, and are traded and bartered.

Carabao are the most important of the Ilocano's domestic animals. They are the primary draft animals in the area, and a farm family without a water buffalo will have to rent one or hire a person to plow their paddy. They are far too valuable to be eaten except when very old or injured, and even then only during very important ceremonies relating to marriages or deaths.

Families tether their water buffalo as close as possible to their homestead in order to protect and care for them. As *carabao* have underdeveloped sweat glands, they are bathed frequently to keep them cool and shaved repeatedly to keep them free from fleas and ticks.

Few of the Good Roots families in Pagudpud can afford to purchase a water buffalo. Instead, the most common practice is to cost share a water buffalo with the aim of ultimately owning an offspring. For example, a relatively poor family will enter into an agreement with a more wealthy family to lease an adult female *carabao*. The lessee is fully responsible for the care and maintenance of the animal. The female water buffalo is bred with an adult male, the cost of which service born by the lessee. When the animal gives birth, the offspring becomes the property of the lessee. The lessee will continue to take care of the water buffalo and its calf until it gives birth again. The second offspring becomes the property of the original owner of the adult female water buffalo. At this point, the agreement may be renewed or terminated. Both parties see themselves as benefiting from this lease relationship.

A variation of this leasing cooperative relationship is also applied to pigs in the communities of San Isidro, Dampig, and Subec.

Because of the presence of numerous rivers and creeks in the area, fresh water fishing is common in the area, and provides farm families with an additional source of food. A few of the families of Subec do some fishing in the nearby South China Sea.

As in most *barangay* in far Northern Luzon, there are also a small number of people who earn some or all of their income by working as teachers, government employees, market vendors, tricycle drivers, small storefront owners, carpenters, craft specialists, and from support from relatives living abroad.

Ilocano social life

Courtship and marriage

Traditional Ilocano courtship and marriage practices are reminiscent of those handed down by the Spanish over a period of 400 years of occupation, combined with a few practices based on aboriginal beliefs. In the past, arranged marriages were common among the Ilocano. Today, arranged marriages hardly exist. Parents, however, want their children to make the best marriage possible so they often offer guidance to their children. The children sometimes interpret this guidance as interference. As remembered by some of the older people in the Good Roots communities, courtship where a young man and his friends would go to a girl's house and sing songs, accompanied by a guitar, was still common in the 1960s. Just a few years ago, young men and women wrote letters to one another as part of the courtship pattern. During the 1970s and 1980s, the best selling books in the Philippines were on how to write love letters. Today, love letters have been replaced with text messaging on a cell phone.

Twenty-five years ago, rural Ilocano culture placed a premium on keeping young men and women apart except in groups in public places. A girl's reputation as a potential mate could be seriously tarnished if she should be so unfortunate as to be put into a situation where she and a young man were alone for any extended period of time. Parents set on forcing a marriage between their son and a girl/woman, for example, have been known to create a situation where the young man and young woman are put in a situation where they have to spend the night alone. This in reality makes the girl unacceptable for any other young man.

In the past, young men and women did not hold hands in public, nor display other kinds of affection such as hugging or kissing. Rural Ilocano behavior between young men and women was predicated on a strong belief that there was to be "no touching" in public. To do so was to shame oneself and the family. It was generally believed that holding hands would lead to embracing one another, and this kind of intimacy would lead to sex. Perhaps because of this "no touch" orientation between boys and girls, overt expressions of affection was common between members of the same sex. The vestiges of this "no touch" behavior can still be seen today in the form of young girls holding hands walking along the road, or young men expressing their affection for one another by holding hands, embracing, or touching a man in a way they would never be allowed to do with a woman.

Today, young men and women meet in school, the market, church, or elsewhere in the community. They hold hands in public, and display other forms of affection in public without social disapproval. They develop friendships, which may lead to courtship and marriage. Parents may try to influence them, but ultimately the decision to marry rest with the young people.

If an Ilocano man and woman decide to marry, the young man will visit the house of the girl's parents and ask permission to plan the wedding. This visit is called *panagudno* in Ilocano. The man's relatives or a spokesman (*panglakayen*) then has a meeting with the girl's parents where a general plan leading to the marriage is worked out, and the boy's parents arrange for the bride-price (*sab-ong*). The amount is based on the wealth of the boy's family, and may be given in cash or in gifts such as land or *carabao*. In addition to the bride-price, the boy's parents assume all the costs for the wedding, including the girl's bridal attire. Discussions of the matter may take several meetings between the parents of the couple. The marriage plans cannot advanced until these issues are settled.

Once financial issues are agreed upon, the date for the wedding is set, and a pastor or priest is asked to officiate at the marriage ceremony. From this period until the wedding, the Ilocano believe that the man and woman to be married should avoid travel as much as possible because betrothed couples are particularly susceptible to misfortune. The future bride should not try on the wedding dress for her friends or family to admire, lest misfortune might lead to the cancellation of the wedding.

A few days before the day of the wedding, the bride and groom, along with their parents, do what is called *agsaksi*—go to the municipal hall and get a marriage license.

The pattern today among the Ilocano of the Pagudpud area is for the couple to be married in a church. A generation ago, many non-Catholics and some Catholics were often married in a civil ceremony performed in the municipal hall by the mayor. In these civil ceremonies, usually the parents of the couple, a few friends, and the *ninong* (male) and *ninang* (female) "sponsors" are present at the wedding. The standard dress for the bride and groom from the more affluent families, of which there are very few in the Good Roots communities, especially when held in a church, is the *traja de boda* for the female and the *barong tagalong* for the male. This wedding dress and man's shirt are made from woven pineapple fiber or raw silk, decorated with elaborate embroidery. The poorer families have the *traja de boda* and *barong tagalog* made from synthetic fabrics or cotton. Marriage for rural Ilocano families is a major life event so no matter how modest the families' income, every attempt is made to stage an impressive affair.

On the day of the wedding, the groom and some of his relatives arrive early at the church. This early arrival is an old Ilocano custom, which some the older men and women jokingly say is to keep the groom from backing out of the wedding. The actual wedding ceremony, if held in the church, is similar to most Christian weddings: a relative "gives" the bride away, a preacher or priest joins the couple in marriage, and there are prayers and songs.

Immediately following the ceremony, the wedding party and guests go to the house of the groom for the reception where an elaborate feast has been prepared by the groom's relatives. The family prepares as much food as it can afford especially of pork. The first activity when the bride and groom reach the house is the *lualo*, a simple but very important ritual where an old woman (usually known for her oratorical abilities) offers a prayer in which she asks for divine guidance and life-long blessings for the newly married couple. After the *lualo*, the couple walk to the *ninangs*, bow slightly, and touch one hand of the *ninangs* against their forehead as a sign of deference and respect. The bride and groom then take a plate each, and accompanied by the *ninangs*, walk among relatives and guests who place money in the plates.

After eating, the *bitor* is held. A native liquor or *basi* is placed on a stand in the middle of the area where people will be dancing. The newly married couple starts dancing and a representative from each family walks to the middle of the dance area and shouts out the name of his or her relatives. The relatives come forward, leave a gift for the couple, and drink a class of *basi* in celebration of the marriage. The *bitor* may last for an hour or more, depending on the number of relatives present.

Finally, the *ninangs* count the money collected in the plates, announce to all present the amount, and then hand it to the groom. The groom then, to the cheering and laughter of the onlookers, hands the money to his wife. The wedding gifts that the guests have brought are then opened.

The newlywed couple usually sleeps at the house where the reception was held.

The typical residence pattern for the newly married Ilocano couple in the Pagudpud area is to stay with the parents of the groom until such time as the couple can afford their own house. Typically they will remain in the area of the groom, but this traditional residence pattern is now dependent as much on economic opportunities as on anything else.

Kinship

The Ilocano term for household is *agkakabbalay*. For the Ilocano, a household is not formed until the time a married couple leaves the house of the man's parents. This usually occurs as soon as a newly married couple can afford to build a house, even if it is on the land of the boy's parents.

The Ilocano term for relative, both consanguineal and affinal, is *kabagyan*.

From the perspective of a male or female Ego, ascending generations include Ego's father (*tatang*) and mother (*inang*), Ego's father's father (*lolo*) and Ego's father's mother (*lola*), and Ego's father's father's father (*lolo ti tuod*) and Ego's father's father's mother (*lola ti tuod*). Ego's father's or mother's siblings and their spouses are *ikit* and *uliteg* respectively. Descending generations include Ego's children (*anak*), whether male or female, Ego's children's children (*apoko*), and children's children's children (*apoko ti tumeng*). Ego's brother is referred to as *kabsat a lalaki* (*manong* if older or *ading* if younger), and Ego's sister is referred to as *kabsat a babai* (*manang* if older and *ading* if younger). Ego's first and second cousins, male or female, are referred to as *kasinsin* and *kapiddua* respectively. Ego's brothers and sister's children are referred to as *kaannakan*.

The Ilocano do not trace affinal relatives beyond the first ascending and descending generations. Regardless of gender, a spouse is *asawa*. A spouse's brother is termed *kayong*, a sister is termed *ipag*. Their spouses are *abirat*. The spouses of Ego's sons and daughters are *manugang*. Ego's father-in-law and mother-in-law is *katugangan* (the former being *katugangan a lalaki* and the latter, *katugangan a babai*).

A summary of Ilocano referential kinship terminology is presented in the kinship charts shown in Figures 2.1 and 2.2.

Birth and growing up as an Ilocano

Having children is a high priority for Ilocano men and women, and a reason stated by many people for getting married. In fact, infertility (usually blamed on the woman regardless of the cause) is a common reason for a couple separating. Consequently, there are many beliefs and taboos associated with pregnancy, birth, and childrearing.

Once a woman learns that she is pregnant, she is cautioned by older women to carry out her daily activities in moderation, especially when traveling, lest the child be hurt. If the woman should leave the house at night (which is not advisable), she should always bring salt and garlic with her to protect her from *aswang* or witches. *Aswang* of the night wander the darkness in search of an opportunity to snatch a child from a woman's womb. Pregnant women never sit on the *agdan* or ladder to the house for fear this may cause the baby to leave the uterus too soon. Pregnant women are careful always to sit on a mat or rug to reduce aid associated with birth. If a pregnant woman sleeps too much during the day, the Pagudpud Ilocano believe the child may be born with *ebbal* (edema) or puffy or bulging face and feet. Pregnant women with long hair extending below their shoulders must always tie it back when they leave the house for fear a snake will be delivered with the baby.

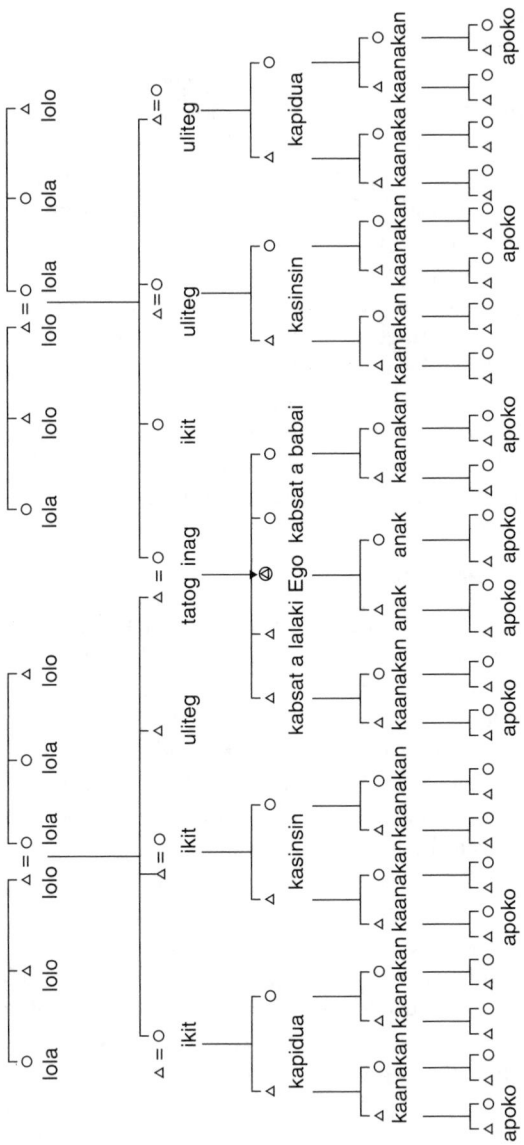

Figure 2.1 Consanguineal terminology of the Pagudpud Ilocano as used for reference or description.

Note
Ego = Male or female.

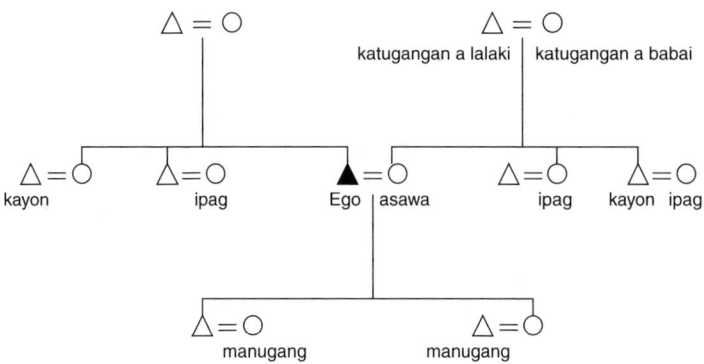

Figure 2.2 Affinal terminology of the Pagudpud Ilocano as used for reference and description.

Note
Ego = Male or female.

If a woman gives birth in a hospital, Western medical practices are followed. If conversely, a woman plans to have the baby at home, as soon as she goes into labor, a local *partera*, a traditional birth attendant (called *hilot* in Filipino) and a midwife are called. When visitors arrive in the house, they are told to avoid stopping or standing on the doorstep for fear the woman will have a difficult delivery. An attempt is made to allow only a very few people in the room with the woman in labor for fear that one of them might be a *sungat*, people who unbeknownst to them have marks on their forehead which could interfere with the delivery process. Among the rural and uneducated, the husband still jumps over his wife three times to bring good fortune during labor. When labor starts, the husband burns old rags under the house to drive away spirits that might impede labor.

For the first fifteen days after delivery, the mother and the baby rest on a *dalagan* or inclined bed. It is believed that this will allow excess blood from the uterus to flow downward. On the first day after birth, she is bathed with water containing guava and pomelo leaves. On the fifth day after birth the mother undergoes *sarab*, a process by which the mother is wrapped in a mat containing charcoal heated guava leaves such that the heat flows directly toward the uterus. She may also sit on hot wood ash wrapped in banana leaves. On the ninth day, she takes a bath where the water is strained through burned rice straw. The *hilot* decides when the mother's birth traumas have healed and her uterus has returned to normal.

During the first fifteen days following delivery, the mother is given a massage with coconut oil by the *hilot* or *partera* to return the mother's muscles to their pre-birth position. Assuming the traditional birth attendant believes the mother has recovered from the birth traumas, the mother will have the *tennab*: a long bath alternating between hot and cold water. At this time, it is safe for her to return to her household chores. It is important, however, that she consume daily a drink made from specific chopped and boiled vines, which are purchased from the nearby Yapayao. It is believed that this drink speeds recovery, and shrinks and cleans the uterus.

Some general Ilocano beliefs and practices, both practical and spiritual, associated with a baby are as follows:

1 As soon as the child is born, the placenta should be wrapped with a pencil in newspaper and buried. This will insure that the baby will grow up to be intelligent.
2 The blanket or clothes in which a newborn is wrapped should be chosen with care because the baby will grow close to the owner of the material as he or she grows older.
3 When a baby is brought out of the house for the first time, the sign of the cross should be marked on the child's face with charcoal, and garlic should be pinned to the clothing. This will protect the child from unseen spirits.
4 Parents should resist the urge to help a child roll over and turn around. This will teach the child not to be dependent on others.
5 Do not let a baby kiss a younger baby. This will cause the older baby not to talk until the younger baby talks.
6 The first piece of money given to the baby should be kept because this will teach the baby to be thrifty.
7 A baby should not be allowed to sleep on his or her stomach on the floor or in a bed, otherwise financial or other hardships will befall the family.
8 When a mother and her baby depart from a house they are visiting, the mother must remember to say something like "let's go baby," to insure the baby's soul does not remain behind.
9 When a baby enters a house for the first time, the owner of the house should touch the baby's forehead. This will insure the baby is comfortable in the new setting.
10 A baby's hair should not be trimmed until his or her first birthday. Otherwise, the baby's life could be shortened.

One of the most significant events in the life of an Ilocano baby or young child is the infant baptism. Because they are Christians, baptism is theologically important to the Ilocano. In addition, for the Ilocano, baptism is equally important socially. This is the time god-parents (*ninong* and *ninang*) are established for the child. Being a godparent is both an honor and a responsibility. It is an honor because it is a public statement that the parents of the child believe the person to be special. It is a responsibility because agreeing to be a godparent means agreeing to be an advocate for the child throughout life, especially in the event of the death of the child's parents.

The transition from childhood to adolescence is the last of the major life events for young Ilocano. Soon after adolescence, young men and women move into the teenage years and the cycle of courtship, marriage, and childbirth starts again.

The Ilocano measure adolescence for girls from the onset of menstruation. The carefree days of childhood end at this time, and the girl starts to assume the responsibilities of a young woman. At the onset of menstruation, the girl sits on the lowest three steps of the ladder or stairs into the house hoping that the period will only last for three days. She learns from the older women that she is prohibited from eating sour food, which can cause blood-clotting and dismenorrhea. During the menstrual period, girls are warned not to sleep during the day or they will develop black circles around their eyes. Finally, girls are discouraged from bathing during menstruation; especially washing their hair, else there might be a sudden stop of the menstrual flow.

The single major event for Ilocano boys at adolescence is what is called *kugit*, circumcision. This ritual occurs at the age of thirteen. The parents of some boys take them to the hospital for this surgical operation, and it is carried out following established Western medical procedures. Other boys go to a native *kugit* specialist who performs the operation with a sharp knife, razor blade, and a wooden mallet. Chewed guava leaves are bound around the wound, and cleaned regularly with boiled banana or guava leaves.

Death and burial

The fatalism of the Ilocano is clearly expressed in their worldview per-taining to the relationship between life and death. A person is born with a particular *gasat* (fate) and dies with the same *gasat*. A person can influence general life events but fundamentally, a person's *gasat* is set at birth: "what will be will be." Death is a tragedy and causes painful grief for loved ones, but the Ilocano believe they can accept death easier than many others because of *gasat*.

Ilocano learn early in life to watch out for omens predicting death. Some of the more common omens are the mooing of cows at dawn, if a black butterfly enters the house at night, when hens cackle incessantly during the night, and if a kingfisher bird flies in a circular fashion around the house. These are signs that the family should exercise caution when leaving the house.

When an Ilocano dies, a fire (called an *atong*) of neatly arranged fuelwood pieces is started in front of the deceased person's house and it remains lit until the funeral. This is to show all people who pass by that a death has occurred in the family.

At death, close relatives (spouse, brothers, sisters, children) wear a white headband (*barabad*) until after the burial, usually nine days after death. Starting with the funeral, the relatives wear black, except at the death of a child, which requires white, until the first anniversary of the death.

Daily prayers are said in the name of the deceased for nine consecutive days after death. In addition, the family holds periodic feasts in honor of the deceased for the following year. The first feast is held on the ninth day after death (*makasiyam*). The next feast is held at one month after death (*makabulan*), followed by another feast at the seventh month (*pitobulan*) after death. The most elaborate feast honoring the deceased is held on the first death anniversary (*makatawen*).

During the waiting period for the funeral, the body rests in a wooden casket, made by relatives or a local person, in the family's house. Some of the more affluent families will purchase a casket from a commercial vendor. Candles are burned 24 hours a day to cast away evil spirits. During this period, friends and relatives come to pay their respects to the deceased.

At the dawn of the day of the funeral, the close relatives kiss the hand of the deceased to show their respect. Later, just before the coffin is carried from the house, a beheaded rooster is thrown in the path that the coffin will pass. This announces to the dead relatives of the deceased that he or she will soon be leaving the earth. The dead relatives should prepare to greet the deceased. The pallbearers must be careful not to allow the coffin to touch any part of the house as they are moving it outside. If this happened, another family member may die soon. Doors and windows in the house are closed as soon as the coffin is carried outside. This is to prevent wandering souls from entering the house. The doors and windows are reopened as soon as the funeral party returns to the house.

Depending on the wealth of the family and the location of the cemetery, the pallbearers may either carry the coffin or the family may rent a hearse (today, usually an old Chevrolet converted into a hearse with a glass enclosed viewing case on the back) to transport it. In most cases, the graveside ceremony is ministered by a pastor or priest. After the graveside ceremony, the relatives and friends of the deceased return to the house where the body was kept to share food, friendship, and sorrow. The expense for the food is borne by the family of the deceased.

The doors and windows of the house of the deceased are kept open for three days and nights after the burial to allow the soul of the deceased to visit the family on the third day after burial.

Ilocano religion

The Ilocano in the greater Pagudpud area belong to a large number of religious denominations, some mainstream, and others, to far less known ones. Adult Ilocano can generally recount the basic doctrines associated with their religion, but beyond that, their religions and ritual practices are syncretistic, reflecting a generalized set of Christian beliefs blended with traditional beliefs.

The most common of the traditional beliefs revolve around protection from malevolent forces and surviving illnesses. For example, amulets or *an-anib* are common among the rural Ilocano. It is believed that ginger will make ghosts sick, and that ghosts are afraid of knives, so many Ilocano carry ginger and knives as protection, especially if out walking at night. Certain roots traded from the Yapayao, and blessed by a priest or pastor on Palm Sunday, are worn to protect people from lightning. Witches or *mannamay* can be are driven away by carrying a small bag of special roots, and salt and garlic serve as general protection from spirits. If a person needs to urinate in an unfamiliar place, he or she will shout "*cayo—cayo,*" "please go away," to drive away unseen, but potentially unfriendly beings. If a man is cutting a tree, he shouts "*dayo—dayo,*" "go away—go away" to frighten away hidden, malevolent creatures. If a man passes by a large dead tree, he will call out "*bari-bari,*" meaning, "please allow us to pass." He does this to pacify the spirits or *anito* (a concept with different meanings in different traditional Filipino cultures) living in the tree.

If an Ilocano should be so unfortunate as to contract an illness or to be injured, there are numerous traditional healers, as well a few physicians trained in Western medicine in the area. Some Ilocano first go to a Western physician for treatment, and then to a local healer. Other people may go first to a local healer and then to a Western physician. If a person receives little or no comfort from one source, the person will try the other source.

There are five basic classes of traditional healers among the Ilocano living in the Good Roots area: (1) *herbolaryo*, (2) *partera* (or *mangablon*), (3) *mammullo*, (4) *mannuma*, and (5) faith healers. *Herbolaryo*, called "quack doctors" in English, are the general practitioners of the traditional medical specialist. These practitioners are particularly knowledgeable of curative herbal compounds, and know how to treat various diseases and aches of their patients. This practice includes treating patients for illnesses that are brought about because of contact with unseen creatures. *Partera* or *mangablon* are women who serve as midwives and generally advise on menstrual disorders, family planning, birth, and postnatal care. *Mammullo* specialize in mending broken bones, treating sprains, realigning dislocated joints, and healing stretched ligaments. The curative techniques are based on the principles of massage. Depending on the practitioner, a variety of concoctions is used as massage oils. Snakebites, dog bite, and other animal and insect bites are treated by specialists known as *mannuma*. The practitioner makes a cut in the wound and sucks out the venom either though the use of a small glass or a piece of *carabao* horn. Finally, faith healers come from the modern world of fundamentalist Christian preachers. These healers follow practices similar to those found among faith healers in the Western world.

Soon after Ferdinand Magellan landed on he Philippine island of Samar in 1521, the first of many native Filipinos were baptized into the Catholic Church: 800 men, women, and children from the island of Cebu. The Catholic priests accompanying the Spanish conquistadors brought and forced Catholicism on the inhabitants of the Philippines. The Spanish military and powerful priests occupied the Philippines until 1898 when American Commodore George Dewey sailed into Manila Bay and destroyed the Spanish fleet. Spain's political influence in the Philippines gradually disappeared, but the power of the Church continued. Consequently, the most dominant religion in the Philippines is Roman Catholicism (generally estimated to be around 85 percent of the total population), including the area of the Good Roots Ilocano.

In the same year that the Philippines received independence from Spain, a Catholic priest named Gregorio Aglipay severed his relationship with Rome, and with other nationalists, formed *Iglesia Filipina Independiente* (IFI), a secular church, the followers of whom are called *Aglipayano*. The ritual of the IFI is similar to that found in the Roman Catholic Church, but the doctrines are markedly different: for example, the Bible is a book of mythology, part fact and part fiction; there are no angels or devils; and Jesus redeemed humanity not with

His death, but with His examples and His teaching. IFI formed an alliance with the Protestant Episcopalian Church of the United States in 1961. In Pagudpud, only a few families are *Aglipayano*.

A religion that is considered by many observers as presenting the major non-Moslem challenge to the Catholic Church in the Philippines is the *Iglesia ni Kristo*. The *Iglesia ni Kristo* in the Pagudpud area is not as strong as elsewhere in the Philippines, but is gaining in strength daily. With spectacular growth since Second World War, mainly because of its social promotions programs, this religion was founded in 1914 by Felix Manalo. He was born a Catholic, and then converted to an Evangelical Christian, a Presbyterian, a Seventh Day Adventist, and a Mormon before founding his own church. In ritual, the religion is patterned on the Mormon Church. In the Church of Jesus Christ of Latter-day Saints, Joseph Smith was the messenger of God, while in the *Iglesia ni Kristo*, Felix Manalo was the messenger of God. Theologically, the *Iglesia ni Kristo* believe that Christ is divine, but is not God. There is no Trinity. Finally, Christ did not die for the sins of all humanity, but for the true believers, the *Iglesia ni Kristo*. In the Pagudpud area, many Ilocano believe that the followers of the *Iglesia ni Kristo* are not "good" Christians because they do not contribute to carolers during Christmas, they do not contribute to town fiestas, members who miss services are punished by the Church elders, and they are only charitable to other *Iglesia ni Kristo*.

There are also small groups of Ilocano *Sakai ni Jehova* (Jehovah's Witnesses), Seventh Day Adventists, Jesus Christ of Latter-Day Saints, and Pentecostal Protestants in the Pagudpud area.

3 The Yapayao

Introduction

The Yapayao, also known as the Apayao or the Iapayao, are a subgroup of the upland minority population of Apayao/Isneg who migrated from the mountain province of Kalinga-Apayao to their present locations in Ilocos Norte. There are two municipalities in northern Ilocos Norte that are predominantly Yapayao; the one *barangay* towns of Adams and Dumalneg (Benner 2001). The thirty-five Good Roots households located in Saliksik, a *barangay* of Dampig, are Yapayao. Dampig, a Good Roots Project village already discussed, is predominantly populated by Ilocano.

The people of Saliksik were forcibly relocated in 1986 to the lowland Yapayao town of Dumalneg situated about 10 kilometers to the southwest. The Philippines government forced this relocation because it believed the families of Saliksik were providing the rebels of the National People's Army (NPA) with personnel, food, and shelter. The Saliksik people slowly started to return to their abandoned farms in 1990.

Popular history, as told by the older Yapayao, and consistent with the writings of Philippine upland specialists (Vanoverbergh 1932; Wilson 1947), holds that as the Spanish moved northward into the Cordillera Central, some Apayao families befriended the Spanish, often trading their lands for hats, cigars, tobacco pipes, and other items brought to the country by the Spanish. Other Apayao families rebelled and fled farther into the mountains. These rebels found refuge near the headwaters of the Bolo River in the province of Kalinga-Apayao. Those families that remained around the headwaters of the Bolo River came to be called the "Apayao," or the "*surong*" (upstream people). The families that moved downstream ("*baba*"), down the Bolo River and the Apayao River, came to be called the

Isneg or Itneg, hence the cultural similarities between the Apayao and the Isneg. The Yapayao of Saliksik trace their history to the upstream Apayao.

The literature on the Apayao or Isneg is scattered and uneven. The anthropologist Felix Keesing (1962) writes briefly about certain aspects of Isneg settlement patterns, economy, kinship, and their religious practices. The Belgian missionary priest Maurice Vanoverbergh (1932, 1936, 1938a,b, 1941, 1950, 1953, and 1953–1955) has been the most prolific student of the Isneg. Other reports on the Isneg, Apayao, or Yapayao are Beyer (1913), Wilson (1947), Faculo (1935), and Scheans (1964).

The community of Saliksik

The Yapayao community of Saliksik consists of 35 households comprising 176 people. Saliksik, isolated from the rest of the community, is a part of the Ilocano *barangay* of Dampig. When the Yapayao returned to Saliksik from Dumalneg, most of the families built temporary houses, made from bamboo and grass thatching situated as close as possible to a stream. When the return migration started, some of the Yapayao walked daily, the 10 kilometers from Dumalneg to Saliksik to work their *kaingins*. Other Yapayao preferred to remain in Saliksik for several days at a time. As time passed, increasingly greater numbers of Yapayao built more permanent houses in Saliksik. They, however, continued to maintain close relations with their relatives in Dumalneg.

Even houses the Yapayao consider permanent are rudimentary in construction, usually remaining useful for only two or three years. Located in or near their *kaingins* or what they call their "*uma*," they are small, one-room structures, with a maximum of seven square meters of floor space, and built on stilts of tree trunks or bamboo above the ground. The walls are made from tree bark or woven bamboo and the roof is usually *cogon* grass (*Imperata cylindrica*) thatching.

Inside the house is a small area where they cook their food (usually over a three-stone hearth), and a place where their cooking and eating utensils are kept. A larger portion or the rest of the interior of the house is where the members of the family eat, sleep, rest, and receive visitors. Their bedding and clothing are placed in one corner of the house, though some keep these tucked in the bamboo ribs supporting the thatched roof. A *putik* (a Chinese jar passed from generation to generation) is a regular feature in a Yapayao house. This jar is a symbol of wealth and kept in one corner of the house.

There is no school in Saliksik, and few of the Yapayao children choose to attend school in the Ilocano section of Dampig. Yapayao parents say that the children are needed in Saliksik to watch over younger children and to work in the *uma*. A common answer by the children to a question about why they do not attend school is "*awan a badbadjong ko*" (I have no dress), spoken in Ilocano, the lingua franca of the area. Only four people living in Saliksik have attended a year or more of high school.

The traditional dress among the Yapayao was *baag* or G-string for the men and *quen* or wrap-around skirt for the women. The *baag* is made from material woven on a back-strap loom and dyed either black or dark blue. The women's skirts were fabricated in this manner but dyed different colors. Only a few old men and women in Saliksik wear these traditional items. Most men wear Western trousers or short pants and a tee shirt, and the women wear Western skirts or dresses. The only times traditional dress can be seen in numbers is during special rituals or during the Dumalneg town fiesta. Tattoos or *gisi* decorate the arms and necks of some of the old men and women.

The Saliksik Yapayao and their neighbors

The people of Saliksik clearly identify with the one *barangay* town of Dumalneg, the predominantly Yapayao town where they were resettled by the Philippines government in 1986. They make regular trips to Dumalneg to attend to various matters. Some Yapayao still have a house in Dumalneg so they go there to check on their property. Some go there to visit relatives. Most Saliksik Yapayao use Dumalneg as a place to buy supplies such as polished rice, *baggoong* (fermented fish sauce), salt, betel nut, and general supplies. There is a Philippine Rural Health Unit in Dumalneg, so some of the people of Saliksik go there to receive free health care and medicines. Finally, they attend Yapayao religious and ritual functions in Dumalneg.

In Dumalneg, the Saliksik Yapayao know they are a part of the majority, and that the Ilocano are the minority. Dumalneg is an old town in Ilocos Norte, dating back to early Spanish occupation. The mayor and the elected officials of the town have long been elected from the ranks of the Yapayao. As such, the Saliksik Yapayao are not treated as second-class citizens or discriminated against by the Ilocano. They enjoy the rights, privileges, services, and amenities available to all the people of the town. Conversely, when interacting with Ilocano outside Dumalneg, the Yapayao tend to be embarrassed at their poverty and lack of education. Many Ilocano consider the Yapayao people a minority population with an inferior culture.

Cooperation between the Yapayao and the Ilocano is heavily dependent on relationships that grow out of economic interdependence. As the Yapayao move back and forth between Saliksik and Dumalneg, they pass through the Ilocano section of the *barangay* of Dampig. Over time acquaintanceships became economic friendships. These relationships most often take the form of what the Yapayao call *abuyog* and *inkaruan*. *Abuyog*, sometimes called *ammuyo*, reflects a situation where members of two different families work in the other's farms on a reciprocal basis. The owner of the farm is responsible for providing snacks and lunch for the workers. *Inkaruan* is an institutionalized relationship between two individuals where one person may pay off a debt to another by working for him. The preference of the Yapayao is to find day-labor jobs so that they can earn cash to purchase household necessities. For these few jobs, they must compete with poor Ilocano.

According to informants, twenty-five years ago, it was unheard of for a Yapayao to marry an Ilocano. Today, occasionally a Yapayao, especially a man, will marry an Ilocana. When this occurs, the choice of whether the marriage is based on Yapayao tradition, or Ilocano tradition with a priest and subject to government regulations, is decided by the couple. The Ilocano practice of *tuptupac* or giving cash gifts to the couple by sponsors and relatives occurs after the ceremony.

Uma cultivation in Saliksik

Because Saliksik is predominantly a mountainous area, upland swidden cultivation accounts for most economic activity. There are few very small parcels of lowland available to the Yapayao. Where this land exists, a few families maintain small rain-fed rice plots, and use *carabao* as draft animals. Fundamentally, the Yapayao of Saliksik, like their ancestors, practice *kaingin* farming.

Including the area given over to *kaingin*, Saliksik covers an area of approximate 30 hectares. Except for the five-year period when the government forced the Yapayao to live in Dumalneg, according to informants, the Yapayao have been doing *kaingin* cultivation in Saliksik since at least the end of the Second World War. Most of Saliksik is secondary forest growth, although on the upper reaches of the mountains, there is still some primary forest growth. The *kaingineros* are reluctant to clear the primary forest areas because of the greater labor requirements, and because of the distance from their houses, and drinking water sources.

The thirty-five Yapayao households in Saliksik cultivate a total of fifty *kaingin*. The average size of a *kaingin* is 3,452 square meters with a total for the area of 17.26 hectares. In general, in households where older children reside, it may farm more than one *kaingin* because of more need for food and an additional labor source.

The Yapayao are the most environmentally conscientious *kaingin* cultivators in the area. In general, they attempt to protect the land by farming an area for only one year, followed by a fallow period of 4–5 years, not as much times as needed to return the plot to healthy secondary growth, but far better than many farmers new to *kaingin* cultivation.

A summary of *kaingin* activities as practiced by the Yapayao of Saliksik during their yearly agricultural seasons follows.

The head of a Yapayao household usually selects the location for the family *uma* during December. If possible, new *kaingins* are located near old ones, making them easier to maintain since houses are situated nearby (Table 3.1). A primary concern when selecting a new site is the thickness of vegetation cover. Little attention is given to the slope of the land or to the number of boulders present. The Yapayao recognize that the thicker the vegetation, the more the organic matter to promote greater yields. An old *kaingin* that has been fallow for at least five years is the preference for the Yapayao. The remaining primary forest in the area is seldom cut by the Yapayao because it is near the upper slopes of the mountains, it is far from their houses, and felling and clearing the large trees is too labor-intensive. Yapayao *kaingins* vary in shape and size. They may be triangular, oblong, rectangular, or irregular in shape and range in size in Saliksik from as small as 447 square meters to as large as 6,266 square meters. In Saliksik, for purposes of maintenance convenience, plot contiguity is important. In some cases, four or more *uma* may be situated side to side.

The Yapayao are far more concerned with rituals associated with farming than are the Ilocano. When the head of the household surveys a piece of land as a potential *uma*, he carries with him pieces of ginger, which serve as offerings to local spirits. In his view, these offerings may prevent him from encountering bad omens during his reconnaissance. Should he encounter a bad omen, it would be unwise for him to select the plot for his *uma*. His yields would be very poor. His misfortune, however, does not prevent another Yapayao from selecting the land for a *kaingin*. Bad omens for the Yapayao when surveying

Table 3.1 *Kaingin* cultivation

Yapayao uma *activity*	Month	Explanation
Malay-laya	December–January	Site selection and rituals to drive evil away
Manaltalon/ magabalasibas	December–January	Marking the site for use
Agraras/maguma	January–February	Cutting small vegetation on the site
Magkallang	March–April	Cutting the large trees
Magrangas	March–April	Cutting felled materials
Sumgab	April–May	Burning the *kaingin*
Magakkat	May	Re-burning debris and cleaning the *uma*
Magballas	May	Weeding the *uma*
Magtabno	May–June	Planting rice
Maglugam/magballas	June–July	Weeding the *uma*
Magbanti/mamugaw	August–September	Protecting the *uma*
Manaligat	October–November	Preliminary harvesting of the *palay*
Magallap	October–November	Finish harvesting the *palay*
Agbilag	November	Drying the *palay*
Agpungo	November	Bundling the reserve seed
Mangipenpen	November	Storing the *palay*
Agbilag	November	Drying the *palay*
Maglugam	November–December	Clearing the *uma* for vegetables
Magmula	February–March	Planting vegetables
Magkuman ku gabit	March	Planting taro (*gabi*)
Magbalolas ku gabit	April	Weeding the *uma*
Magallap	May–June	Harvesting *gabi*

land for a *kaingin* are, as follows:

1 If he should encounter any species of snake, he should leave the area.
2 Seeing a Monitor lizard is a sign that the yields will be poor or that a family member may become ill.
3 Encountering a Kingfisher bird is a sign that disaster may befall his *uma*.
4 The cries of a deer is interpreted as being told to look elsewhere for a *kaingin* plot.

In many cases, during the reconnaissance, a man may place a piece of ginger on a stick or small tree in the plot to test the potential of the plot. If the ginger is still there after two days, then it is safe to use the area as an *uma*. This is a traditional Yapayao practice, although it is only the older Yapayao that presently follow the practice. Other Yapayao in Saliksik simply clear a small portion of the plot with a machete. This marks the plot as belonging to someone.

About a week after the site has been marked, usually in January, the members of the household, except small children, start the process of clearing the undergrowth—brush, vines, and small shrubs—on the site. Often this involves the exchange of labor. If a household helps its neighbor clear the underbrush, the neighbor is obligated to reciprocate with like services. If a man has no wife or the household is very small, he may have to clear the underbrush of his neighbor so that his neighbor's wife or older daughter can help him plant. Yapayao women assume primarily responsibility for planting the *kaingins*. Depending on the size of the *kaingin*, clearing the underbrush may take from a few days to several weeks. Often, the thickness of the underbrush requires 2 or 3 times of clearing.

After the cleared underbrush has dried, work groups consider their actions toward large trees. Often, rather than felling large trees, the workers top the trees, and cut the limbs into the smaller pieces. After this process is completed, the *kaingin* plot appears a shambles of dried leaves, bushes, shrubs, and cut limbs, all lying at the base of the topped trees left standing.

The high temperatures and hot sun of April, the peak of the dry season, dries the felled debris, and prepares it for firing. Timing is critical at this juncture in the cultivation cycle. If a family misjudges the onset of the rainy season, it could be difficult to re-burn the debris that did not burn well during the first burning, which would affect the planting and growing period. In an ideal world, the Yapayao prefer to do one or two burnings over a period of a day or two, followed by afternoon showers a day or two later. This allows the area to cool, making cleaning, and spot re-burning much easier. Tree limbs or smaller trees that did not burn well are cut, gathered, and used later as fuelwood or for fence construction. The family cleans the area very carefully so that the thin-coated weed seeds will germinate quickly and spread rapidly.

The afternoon showers and tropical heat of early May contribute greatly to the growth of weeds in the *uma*. About a week after the rains commence, the plot is dotted with emerging weeds. This is especially the case if the area has been fallow for four or five years. When the weeds grow to around 6–8 inches tall—making them easier to grab by hand and pull from the ground—the family starts its final cleaning of the *uma*. This may take up to a week: weeds are pulled, maybe some minor re-burning is done, and the area is swept clean of debris in preparation for planting the rice.

The arrival of the rainy season, usually in late May, is a joyful occasion for the Yapayao. It marks the beginning of the growth of the most important food source for the Yapayao. The soil is moist and relatively easy to work. By tradition, Yapayao women take a leading role in the planting of rice. The women of household often enter into a labor-reciprocal relationship. If a man has no woman in his household, he may trade his labor for work of a different sort for the labor of the wife of his neighbor.

Preparing the rice seeds for planting is not an easy task. Instead of threshing small bundles of *palay* against a hard object to remove the hulls, the women foot-thresh the grain so that it may be gently separated from the stem. The result of this more gentle procedure is less damaging to the grain, which allows for a higher percentage of the grain to emerge from the soil after it is planted.

The basic planting implement used by Yapayao women is a dibble or pointed stick made from hardwood. It is called a *gaddang* in Yapayao. The general technique followed by the women is to thrust the dibble into the ground with one hand, move it about so that a small hole about four inches deep is created, then with the other hand, reach into a bag tied at her waist, take 5–8 rice grains, and drop them into the hole.

Rice planting starts in the middle of the *uma* and the women work in a circle until the end of the day. If it takes more than one day to plant the *kaingin*, the workers are not required to follow this pattern. They usually start at the lower edge of the *kaingin* and work upward. The Yapayao believe that they should not plant in a downward direction because this would make it easier for insects to attack the grain in the holes.

Soon after the rice is planted, the Yapayao turn to planting other cultigens in the *uma*. Just as a tropical or subtropical forest is a generalized ecosystem, so too is a Yapayao *uma*. Like many slash-and-burn cultivators, the Yapayao plant cultigens in their swiddens that will mature at different rates. This allows them to harvest foods over a relatively long period. Soon after the rice planting, the most common cultigens planted after the rice planting are okra, beans, luffa gourd, and ampalaya (bitter melon). Okra and beans are generally planted along the edges of the *uma*. Luffa and bitter melon, both climbing vine plants, are planted at the base of stumps or topped trees.

Ritual is not a major part of Yapayao planting unless a family member has had the misfortune to dream about a dead relative. If this should occur, rice and other foods are offered to the spirits of the deceased to insure that the spirits will not molest the *uma*, which could cause a poor yield. If the family can afford it, a chicken may be sacrificed before the planting. If the family is very poor, a boiled egg may be offered as a substitute for a chicken to the spirits. A more common practice is to place a *mamaen* (a mixture of betel nut, lime, and water) in one of the corners of the *uma*.

Weeds compete with cultigens for sunlight, water, and soil nutrients. Weeds also harbor pests and diseases. Consequently, weeding is a critical feature of the Yapayao farming cycle. By the time the *palay* has grown to a height of around eight inches, the weeds will have emerged from the soil. Using a small hoe-like implement called a *ballas*, the Yapayao start weeding sometime in late June or early July. Weeding is a slow activity, especially if the weeds are thick, and takes a party of four about two weeks to complete the weeding of a half hectare *kaingin*. This first weeding is the most important for a successful yield, but additional weeding is necessary from time to time as weeds continue to grow in the *uma*.

The Yapayao spend a considerable amount of time protecting their crops from pests and diseases. The farmers must constantly stay alert for birds, rats, wild pigs, and the occasional monkey or domestic animal. This is another reason the Yapayao prefer their *kaingins* to be located near their houses. If the *uma* is located more than a kilometer from the house, usually a Yapayao man will construct a temporary house (*sigay*) where he or a caretaker can stay from time to time. The most common objects placed in the swiddens to frighten pests are scarecrows, white rags tied to sticks, colored pieces of cellophane that flutter in even the slightest breeze. Traditionally, sharpened bamboo spikes were sometimes placed around the *uma* to protect it from wild animals, but with growing competition for limited resources, and the gradual disappearance of wild pigs, deer, monkeys, and many birds, the Yapayao now feel this practice to be redundant. Some of the Yapayao construct makeshift bamboo and stick fences around abandoned swiddens because even if left to fallow, for a few years there are still a few cultigens growing in the swidden.

The time of the rice harvest is an important period for the Yapayao, not only because of the importance of rice as the staple food, but because it is a time when rituals must be performed as an expression of gratitude to the spirits for the harvest, and the harvest must be done in a specified manner. Food offerings are initially made to ancestral spirits as a means of thanksgiving, and asking for aid in a bountiful harvest. The actual harvesting of the rice is considered by the Yapayao to be a ritual act. Failure to complete either procedure could cause the family to suffer misfortune. The harvest starts with the head of the house taking a small, single-bladed knife (*rakem*), and then cutting *palay* stalks about eight inches long until they constitute a bundle about two inches in diameter. He then proceeds to place the bundle in the granary where it will not be handled until the following planting season. This act is an offering to the spirits, and an insurance that there will always be some seed for the next year.

After the head of the household has completed this rite, the rest of the family gathers at the edge of the *uma*, and proceeds to harvest in a circular pattern. They create a strip about a meter wide, while circling toward the center of the *uma*. Two or three people cut the *palay* stalks about eight inches long and give a two inch bunch to a trailing person who ties the bundle with a piece of split bamboo. Only one person does the tying to insure uniformity in bundle size.

If additional labor is needed for the harvest, compensation is not based on reciprocity as is usual among the Yapayao. Instead, workers are remunerated with *palay*, either at a fixed daily rate or with a share at completion of the harvest.

Post-harvest handling and storage are critical features of the rice harvest. If the *palay* is not properly dried, it can germinate too easily. It is also very susceptible to mold. To insure safe drying and storage, the bundles of harvest *palay* are stacked so that the grain is exposed to the sun for two days. The bundles are turned, exposing the other side of the grain, for another two days. Reserve seeds for the next year's planting are dried for an additional two days.

The *palay* is tied for convenience of drying, storage, and use. The *palay* is initially tied to form a small bundle measuring two inches in diameter at the stems. One small bundle is called a *pusot*. Six *pusot* equals one larger bundle or a *pungo*. Two *pungo* equal one *baar*, and ten *baar* equal one *uyon*. The bundles intended for consumption are placed on the floor of the granary, and the reserve seeds for planting are hung from the truss of the granary.

As is usually the case among the hill people of Northern Luzon, the most important structure for the Yapayao family is the granary. Often, granaries are better built than houses. The granary is constructed in the *kaingin* nearest the family's house for ease of use and protection. Yapayao granaries are small, only about four square meters of floor space, and built on stilts around three feet high. The walls are made from dried tree bark and the roof is *cogon* grass. About a foot below the floor, encircling the support post, are rat guards made from galvanized sheet metal. Traditionally, the rat guards were made from wood.

Other sources of food and income

Mainly because of increasing competition for limited resources from lowlanders, a minor source of food for the Saliksik Yapayao comes from hunting wild boar, deer, wild chicken, and birds. Boar and deer are tracked with dogs and killed with a spear. Wild chickens and birds are trapped.

More significant as a source of food for the people of Saliksik are two streams that run through the community. The streams are abundant in fresh water shrimp, crabs, and a variety of fish. The Yapayao catch these creatures by hand, with traps, with hook, and by using nets. Most of the daily catch is consumed by the family although occasionally, if there is a particularly good catch, a Yapayao may carry it into the lowlands and trade it for needed supplies.

The Saliksik Yapayao generate a little income each year through mat weaving. The mats are either sold or traded to lowlanders. Some of the men work as day laborers for the lowland Yapayao or Ilocano.

Finally, household income in Saliksik is supplemented from the proceeds generated by illegal logging (discussed in detail later).

Yapayao social life

Sociopolitical organization

From the perspective of socio-political interaction, although the Yapayao living in Saliksik are technically members of the predominantly Ilocano *barangay* of Dampig, and as such have voting privileges in Dampig, their close relationships are with the Yapayao living in Dumalneg. As noted, the people of Saliksik and the people of Dumalneg share a common Yapayao ancestry. Saliksik is a Yapayao minority *purok* (a definable neighborhood or village) of the *barangay* of Dampig, one several definable communities of the Municipality of Pagudpud, Ilocos Norte. The political officers of Dampig are a *Barangay* Captain and seven councilors, elected at large. The elected officials of the one-*barangay* town of Dumalneg are ethnically Yapayao.

Whenever possible, settling disputes between Yapayao individuals or families is done outside the political structure of the Philippine government. Larger Yapayao communities or groups of smaller Yapayao communities have a jurisprudence council composed of elder men (*panua wen*). The *panua wen* is headed by a primary elder (*sarikampo*), whose authority is derived from his age and his wisdom, and to a lesser extent his oratorical ability. Before the Second World

War, the *sarikampo* also had to have led many successful head-taking expeditions. The primary function of the council is to mediate disputes between Yapayao individuals, and families, and to levy fines or other penalties for social transgressions. For example, if a man and woman are accused of committing adultery, both parties come before the council of *panau wen*. The council listens to the case, and then imposes the fine. The general punishment for this offense is both the man and the woman are cut on the arm or leg with a knife such that a scar forms when healing, thus marking the person with the sign of adultery. The male is further penalized by being forced to pay the woman's husband a *mariapa* (a small Chinese jar), or cash. The council of *panau wen* also mediates family disputes, quarrels, theft, and general disagreements.

If the disagreement is between a Yapayao and an Ilocano, mediation is handled by the local Philippine courts.

Informants say that the last time a head was taken by a Yapayao was during the Second World War. Several Philippines hill tribes, including the Yapayao, worked as mercenaries for both the Japanese and the Americans/Filipinos during this war. Heads or ears were presented to the Allied Forces as proof of the kill. This fostered a short-lived rebirth of head-taking activity.

Although the Yapayao no longer take heads, the mystique of the practice, especially as perceived by lowlanders, persists today, and conditions the Ilocano view of the Yapayao and the Yapayao's view of themselves. Many Ilocano still think of the Yapayao as hill peoples who haven't yet been fully "civilized." The Yapayao take pride in their cultural heritage.

Traditionally, the taking of a head came about for two reasons: for individuals and families to avenge a wrong (within or outside the tribal group), or as a way for a man to prove his worth as a Yapayao. Only men who had taken several heads could attain the rank of *panau wen*, and become a member of the council.

After a man killed a person, he took a special axe, called an *aliwa*, and severed the head from the body. A day or two after the head is cut, it is presented to the *sarikampo*. A celebration (called a *patong*, the general term for ritual in Yapayao) is held. For the celebration one or more pigs are butchered, there is dancing, drinking, and general frivolity. The highlight of the evening is for the man who took the head to dance with the head for all to see, and to recount his head-taking exploits. After the *patong*, the skin is removed from the head and given to the most important *bolo* (machete) maker in the community. The skull is placed on a rack inside the house of the *bolo* maker. His house is called *ballawa* in Yapayao (meaning a place of skull preservation).

Courtship and marriage

In the past, courtship among the Yapayao was an unimportant activity. Marriages were arranged by families, often when their children were only 2 or 3 years old. The marriage was consummated when the girl reached the age of 12 or 13, and the boy reached the age of 14 or 15. Presently, a few marriages are arranged, while most young Yapayao men and woman go through a courtship process that is a reflection of generalized lowland courtship patterns. After courtship, Yapayao parents have an important role in making arrangements leading to a marriage.

Unmarried Yapayao girls say that what they want in a husband is a man who is industrious. If questioned more closely, however, some of them say that if the man is not industrious, he must at least be handsome, and they hope he can be changed. Young men say they want a woman who is hard-working, who is good at *kaingin* cultivation, and whom he believes will bear him many children.

Just before the marriage (whether by arrangement or courtship), the young man and his family present a bride-price to the parents of the girls and her near relatives, consisting of *manding* (a valuable antique Chinese bead), *aliwa* (head axe), *quen* (skirt), and *ules* (blanket). Some of the more economically successful Yapayao may give a *carabao*, or a small parcel of land for the bride-price.

Presenting the bride-price to the girl's parents is accompanied by a small, but important pre-marriage ritual. The boy's parents or other relatives present the girl's parents and other relatives some gifts and betelnut (*bua*) wrapped in a piece of cloth. If the girl's parents believe the bride-price is too low or something else is wrong, they will cut the cloth-wrapped betelnut, rendering the negotiations over for the evening. The boy's parents can return to the girls' parents at another time. If the girl's parents accept the small gift from the boy's parents, both parties immediately have a *biraw* (chewing and sharing of betelnut). The date for the marriage is set, and the young man and woman celebrate the coming marriage by sleeping together that night.

The Yapayao marriage ceremony is a simple affair. The young man and woman, along with their relatives, assemble at the house of the boy's parents. The ceremony is officiated by a *panau wen* known for his oratorical abilities. The ritual performed is called *inapugan*. A child, either male or female and around the age of 5–8, stands before the young couple holding lime (*apug*) and betelnut in the palm of his or her hand. The groom takes either the betel nut or lime from the child's hand and the bride takes the item that remains, symbolically acknowledging that the two (betelnut and lime) and the couple go together. Immediately following the *inapugan*, there is a feast consisting of rice, pork, and vegetables, the cost of which is borne by the girl's relatives, and takes place at the house of the girl's relatives. After eating and drinking, the girl's parents and other relatives return to the house of the boy's parents where they receive final payment of the bride-price. That night, the newly married couple sleeps in the house of the parents of the boy, and then go to the girl's parents house the next day. If a Yapayao marries an Ilocano, the *inapugan* is not held.

By tradition, when a Yapayao couple married, a matrilocal residential pattern is followed. The young man leaves his household of origin, and moves in with his wife and wife's family. This lasts for a few years, until such time that the couple has children, and is ready to establish their own household. At this time, the couple establishes a new household in a new or nearby location. If the couple has a surviving parent, he or she may live with the couple, as would widowed uncles or aunts, or children with disabilities.

Some Yapayao still follow this cultural pattern while others choose to establish a new household soon after marriage.

In general, monogamy is the most common form of marriage among the Yapayao. If, however, the man chooses to take a second wife, he may do so if his wife approves. If the wife does not approve, he may take a second wife, but he must compensate his wife's relatives, the amount decided by the council of *panau wen*.

Incompatibility is cited by Yapayao as reason for divorce. If a man and woman decide to divorce, the bride-price is not returned. If the marriage resulted in no children, the little wealth they have accumulated together is divided, and the man leaves the house. If there are children, they remain with the mother and her relatives, as does any accumulated wealth. The man leaves the house.

Relatives and kinship

A feature of Yapayao kinship, similar to other hill peoples of Northern Luzon, is based on what has been called a "personal kindred" (Eggan 1960). The Yapayao personal kindred is a bilateral group of kinsmen surrounding a particular individual. Ideally, it embraces all of a person's descendants from four generations, extending laterally to include third cousins. Today, this is generally beyond the socially effective range, so lateral numeration is dependent upon a person's genealogical knowledge.

In addition, the Yapayao kinship system in Saliksik is generational and symmetrical. Consanguineal kinship is most important, and from the perspective of the community, marriage is a formal alliance between kindred. When a couple marries, the kinship base is expanded and the parents of the newly married couple become co-parents-in-law. This is especially important when a child is born to the new couple. In Yapayao society, a kinsman is by definition an ally and friend. The more kinsmen a person has, the more allies he has.

The *agkokobon* or household is the most important economic unit in the village. Farming and other income-generating activities are the responsibility of and determined by the members of the house.

The Yapayao term for "relative," whether consanguine or affinal is *kabagyan*. From the perspective of a male or female Ego, ascending generations include Ego's father (*ama*) and mother (*ina*), through great-great-great-grandfather and grandmother (*kakay na buwal* or *apo na buwal*). Mother's and father's siblings and their spouses are referred to as *ama* or *ina*, and great-grandparents are referred to as *kakay na buwal or apo na buwal*. Descending generations include Ego's children (*anak*), whether male or female, and Ego's great (*apoko*) and great-great-grandchildren (*apoko na buwal*). The children of Ego's father's brother or sister, and Ego's mother's brother or sister, are referred to as *kapinsan*. Second cousins are *kapidua*. The term for brother or sister is *gayam*. The spouse of a *gayam is kayong*.

The Yapayao do not trace affinal relatives beyond the first ascending or descending generation. Regardless of gender, a spouse is *asawa*. The brother or sister of a spouse is *kayong*, while their spouse is *abirat*. The sons or daughters of a sister or brother are *manugang*. Ego's father-in-law or mother-in-law is *katugangan* (the former being *katugangan nina lakay* and the latter, *katugangan nina baket*).

A summary of Yapayao referential kinship terminology is presented in the kinship charts shown in Figures 3.1 and 3.2.

Religion and ritual

The term that most accurately describes religion among the Yapayao in the Saliksik–Dumalneg area is "syncretism." For the most part, rituals are based on tradition, conditioned by Christian beliefs. The Christian influence comes primarily from the Roman Catholic Church, the non-denominational *Eglesia Filipina Independiente*, and the "back to nature" Christian based Space Ship 2000 (formerly the

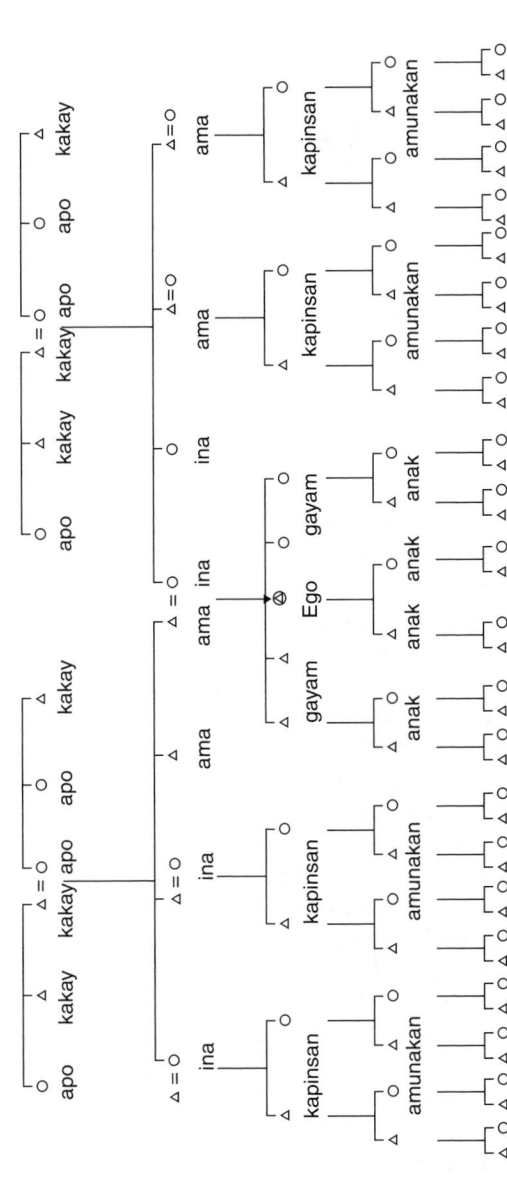

Figure 3.1 Consanguineal terminology of the Saliksik Yapayao as used for reference or description.

Note
Ego = Male or female.

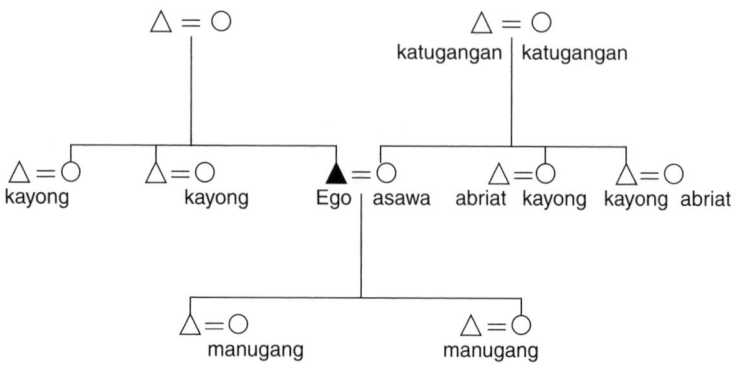

Figure 3.2 Affinal terminology of the Saliksik Yapayao as used for reference and description.

Note
Ego = Male or female.

Lamplighters). The view held by most Yapayao regarding God, heaven, and hell is fundamentally Christian. God lives in heaven, is all powerful, and when a person dies, the spirit ascends to heaven or descends to hell, depending on his deeds while alive. Some Yapayao believe that God does not live in heaven but within each person. God lives in a good person. The Devil lives in a bad person. Other Yapayao believe that when a person dies, the soul goes into the sky, only to return to earth. Finally, a few Yapayao are unwilling to commit to a specific belief. They acknowledge a supreme being of some sort, but say they don't know anything about it. These people say that the fate of the soul at death is unknown. Regardless of a Yapayao's view of gods and the afterlife, spirits are an important part of Yapayao culture and must be appeased with numerous offerings.

The Yapayao identify three classes of spirits: (1) *kaibaan*, (2) *aswang* (sometimes called *biruka*), and (3) *minatay a nabaybay-an*.

Kaibaan appear during the day or night in the form of a beautiful young woman or handsome man, both of whom are heavily decorated with tattoos. These spirits live in the forest, especially near trees that cluster together. If a person should be so unfortunate as to see a *kaibaan*, he or she will suffer immensely. The victim would most definitely lose his or her hair. In addition, the victim could contract physical ailments such as edema, leprosy, joint pains, or become paralyzed. If a person starts to display symptoms of this nature, it is generally assumed he or she has seen *a kaibaan*, and a curing ceremony must be held. Otherwise, the victim would die. In addition to making food offering to both the *kaibaan* and ancestral spirits, the victim will be washed with herbal water (*digos nga ruot*).

Aswang is a human-like creature that metamorphoses from a human into a half-human and half-black crow during the night. This nocturnal creature is evil, and behaviorally uses its beak as a blood-sucking instrument. It wanders the forest during the night looking for children so that it may devour the liver of the child by sucking the blood from the child's body. A person, especially a child, who becomes thinner and thinner, is suspected of having been exposed to *aswang*. If a Yapayao medical practitioner suspects the child has been exposed to *aswang*, a curing ceremony is held.

All deceased Yapayao have spirits who are to be honored, acknowledged, and fed from time to time by their living relatives. All spirits are potentially dangerous. *Minatay a nabaybay-an*, spirits of bodies buried under the house and abandoned by their relatives, are especially menacing. Even minimal contact with these spirits can cause accidents or cause illnesses. Consequently, ancestral spirits are to be honored, fed, and feared.

Spirits are so dangerous to the Yapayao that even during ceremonies designed to cure illness and exorcize spirits, all the participants and onlookers, wear amulets or *an-anib* as protection from spirits. Without the *an-anib*, a person can be possessed (*mabalsan*) by a spirit. If this should happen, the Yapayao believe the person will die.

Anito, a common concept among the mountain peoples of Northern Luzon, with a wide range of meanings from a specific ritual to god-like spirits, is equally a common concept among the Yapayao. For the Yapayao, *anito* is a ritual performed to pacify and eventually drive away spirits and to cure illness or injury. This is usually a small ceremony performed by a medium for a family. It is an important Yapayao ritual but it is far less elaborate than some rituals. An *anito* may be performed in association with other rituals.

The most elaborate Yapayao rituals are called *patong*, the most important of which are: *patong a saong, patong a tugot, patong a parangpang*, and *patong a sinang-at*. A *patong* involves dancing, gong-playing, oratory, the ritual killing of pigs, chickens, or a small dog, and the feeding of friends and relatives. The purpose of a *patong* is to realize a social end, but it is also a social event, and often takes on the character of a celebration.

A *patong a sapong* is a celebration held each year by relatives of a deceased person, which is to honor the deceased and to dissuade spirits of the dead from entering the world of the living. The *patong a tugot* is effectively a marriage feast. Both visitors and spirits are fed rice and pork, and specific rites are performed which serve to benefit the newly married couple. When a man or woman makes a commitment to understudy a *durarakit*, an established, respected, and skilled healer and medium, a *patong* a *parangpang* is held to initiate the neophyte into the world of the Yapayao medium. It will take the understudy many years to acquire the knowledge of ritual and medicine to become an accepted *durarakit*. The understudy may have to wait for a *durarakit* to die before he or she attains this position in Yapayao society. A *patong a parubuat* is held when a *durarakit* dies, a *panau wen* dies, or a local political official such as the mayor dies. Finally, a *patong a sinang* is held when someone becomes very ill.

The complexity and character of a Yapayao *patong*, a *patong a sinang*, is illustrated in the following account.

Manulito, a Yapayao man of 45 years of age, went into the forest one day and to his misfortune, he chanced upon an evil spirit. He immediately returned to his house, got some cooked rice and vegetables, and returned to the forest. As he was about to make a food offering to the spirit, a large branch of a tree fell on his head and he was knocked unconscious. He returned home without feeding the spirit. He became dizzy and dazed to the point that his family took him to the nearest Philippine public hospital. The Western trained physicians at the hospital were unable to cure Manulito so his relatives took him home.

Manulito's family decided that in order to save his life, they needed to hold a *patong a sinang*, so they contacted Dumagi, an old and respected healer and medium, and asked him to officiate the *patong*. The chief medium is called *durrarakit na mangngagas* (the original healer) in Yapayao. Because Manulito was very ill, the *patong* needed to be a major event, Dumagi asked two women to assist him, both of whom are healers (*arupagan*), one almost equal in status with Dumagi, and the other, more an understudy.

During the morning of the first day of the *patong*, Dumagi placed in the hands of the two *arupagan*, Hermogilda and Labnay, a bracelet, endowed with mystical power, made from old and valuable beads of Chinese origin. The two women unrolled a woven mat and cleared it. The Yapayao believe they need to prepare a mat for the evil spirits who wish to be comfortable. The assistants then killed a puppy as a sacrificial offering to the spirits, and hung it at the door of the house. Gongs and drums were played loudly to attract the evil spirits to the house.

That evening, a large native pig, and a chicken were tied at the door of the house as symbolic payment to the evil spirits. A large crowd of

Yapayao assembled at the house. Manulito's male relatives picked him up from a bed in front of the house on which he was lying and moved him into the house. The gongs and drums started to play loudly. Dumagi and his two assistants took the spirit mat and started moving it around Manulito, often purposefully touching him with the mat. In time, Manulito was wrapped in the mat, and then unwrapped. Manulito, held upright by two male relatives, was washed by the two assistants with water that has been blessed by Dumagi. The blessed water is to wash the evil spirits away. After the washing, Dumagi dipped a coconut raceme into the water pot and sprinkled water on Manulito's head. The three healers took a banana leaf, made it into a flat roll, and wrapped it around their head as a headband. The senior healer placed a banana leaf in a corner of the house that serves as an *an-anib* or amulet for the family. A bundle of upland rice (*maliket*) was placed in a basket, and a small saucer filled with oil was placed in an earthen pot. A string was placed in the oil and lighted.

Dumagi's senior *arupagan* untied her long hair, and called two women relatives of Manulito to stand guard before her. Each was holding a spear that is to protect all the participants from evil spirits. The ailing and possessed Manulito was placed before Dumagi and his senior assistant. He was wrapped in native cloth. The lighted saucer of oil was placed in front of Manulito to help drive the evil spirits away. Manulito's wife sat beside Manulito holding the basket of upland rice above her head. Dumagi and his assistants took two shells and shook them at Manulito in an attempt to drive the evil spirits away. They then took some of the rice and sprinkle it on the head of the sick man and his wife, hoping to appease the evil spirits. Dumagi and his assistant then removed the rice grains from the head of Manulito and his wife. As soon as this was completed, the gongs and drums began to play, first slowly and then loudly and rapidly. Dumagi and his assistants began to dance. The dance becomes more frenetic. The dancers began stomping their feet in the hope of frightening away the spirits. Dancing and gong-playing went on for almost an hour before the evening quieted, and the participants turned to sleep or slow drinking.

The following morning a large pig was sacrificed (one-third given to Dumagi and his two assistants) and prepared as a noon meal for all the people at the ceremony. Manulito was sprinkled with "holy" water several more times during the day. Throughout the day, there was continuous stomp-dancing. Different people took turns playing the drums and gongs.

Manulito died a few days after the *patong a sinang*. The speculation among the Yapayao is that he had accidentally killed an unseen evil spirit while collecting fuelwood along the Bolo River. If this was the case, no amount of ceremonial cleansing could have saved him from death. A common Yapayao saying is: "if you owe a life, you must pay with a life."

4 Measuring the forest

Introduction

Within the Philippines, it is the means by which human populations interact with nature, mainly through population growth and the misuses of technology, which can account for the extent of deforestation. This observation, however, is a dramatic oversimplification of this ecological reality. Fundamentally, regardless of the technology used or the cultural perceptions followed, human–nature interaction must be examined within the context of the ever changing cultural and environmental variables.

In order to identify the impact the various modes of human–nature interaction contributed to the destruction of the forest, the research team first had to answer the question of how many trees are utilized and/or destroyed each year due to technological and cultural factors in the four Good Roots research communities.

Collecting data

In order to determine accurately the extent of tree loss in the Good Roots area, the research and development team employed several labor intensive data-gathering techniques. Because the primary concern of this phase of the Good Roots research was the impact of culture on nature, the first question the team needed to address was: what is the universe of nature in the area or how many trees are there in a primary forest growth area and how many trees are there in a secondary growth area? Only then could the questions of how many trees are lost due to cultural factors—namely *kaingin* farming, charcoal utilization and making, fuelwood consumption, illegal logging and minor construction activities—be measured and placed within the perspective of nature.

To ascertain the volume and number of trees in a primary forest, the research team (already very familiar with the area) surveyed the land surrounding the study villages and identified through visual observation "typical" primary forests. The primary forest cover adjacent to or within 3–5 kilometers of the communities of Subec, Dampig, San Isidro, and Saliksik are generally 400 meters above sea level. Almost all land below 400 meters has already been significantly affected by human intervention, that is, the land below 400 meters from the foothills to the South China Sea, a straight-line distance of 8 kilometers, has been under paddy, dry field plow and *kaingin* cultivation for decades. Further inland, beyond the first series of foothills, there is insignificant human occupation and the primary forest falls below 400 meters on the eastern slopes of the foothills.

After "typical" primary forest areas were identified, ten sample plots of 10 meters by 10 meters (100 square meters) were marked for survey. Within each of the 10 meter plots, the common species of trees were identified and all trees were marked as less than 2 centimeters in diameter, between 2 centimeters and 49 centimeters diameter at breast height, or above 50 centimeters in diameter at breast height. All wildlings or trees below 2 centimeters were counted. All other trees in the ten sample plots were counted and measured (main trunk and all branches more than 2 centimeters in diameter) and the measurements were calculated in terms of cubic volume ($0.7854 \times$ diameter squared $\times$ length). This activity involved hundreds of measurements and calculations and resulted in a detailed measurement of wood volume and number of trees in primary forest growth.

The same measuring techniques that were applied in primary forest areas were also utilized for secondary growth areas except that the sample consisted of three plots, measuring 10 meter by 10 meter.

Data on tree loss due to *kaingin* activity was collected by first measuring all fifty of the *kaingin*s in Saliksik, the project community exclusively practicing this form of agriculture. A 10 percent sample of the *kaingin*s was taken in Subec, Dampig and San Isidro where *kaingin* activity is minor. Because all of the *kaingin*s in the project area are in secondary forest covered lands where there is a 4–5 year fallow period, three plots 10 meter by 10 meter of secondary growth covered land were marked for measurement. The same techniques used in measuring primary and secondary forests were applied to the secondary growth covering previous *kaingin*s. Wildlings below 2 centimeters were counted, not measured, and there were no trees greater than 50 centimeters in diameter in the *kaingin* areas except some that were long dead. Knowing the exact amount of land devoted to *kaingin* activity and the volume/trees in secondary forest growth areas allowed for a calculation of the number of trees lost due to *kaingin* activity.

Determining the number of trees lost to charcoal-making was derived from an actual measure of the daily consumption of charcoal in the *barangay* of San Isidro, the only charcoal-making community in the study. The research team discussed the issue with the charcoal-makers, a measurement of daily charcoal consumption was taken, and the species, number, and volume of trees used in making the charcoal was established. Knowing the cubic volume of the various species used in charcoal-making (from the detailed measurements on the forests) allowed for a calculation of the number of trees lost due to this activity.

During the household census at the beginning of the Good Roots Project in 1991, household heads were queried as to how many sticks of fuelwood they consumed daily for cooking and heating. Informant responses were verified by the research team through random measurements of species used as fuelwood by diameter and length over a period of a year. Fuelwood stockpiles were measured and converted into cubic volume by species. Once daily consumption was determined, the data were measured against the volume of fuelwood in specific species in the forest in order to determine the number of trees lost as fuelwood.

Because of the clandestine nature of illegal logging, gathering data on this activity was both sensitive and difficult. In the Good Roots area, illegal logging is done by small teams of 5–7 men using only chain saws, axes, machetes and digging bars. Illegal logging, while commercial in character, is not of the type frequently described in the popular press where thousands of hard-wood trees are cut by well-financed logging companies, and destroyed by heavy construction machinery. There are fifteen teams of illegal loggers operating in the project area and at least one member of all fifteen teams were interviewed as to the species and number of trees each team cuts during a year. The illegal logging sites were visited by the research team and where possible, the size of trees cut and the size of the processed logs were measured. Given this information, the actual number of trees felled through illegal logging was calculated.

The amount of wood used for minor construction of makeshift or temporary houses, granaries and incidental sheds was determined by the actual measurement of the woods in 15 percent of the structures in the *kaingin*s. Data on this activity were limited to *kaingin*s because it is only in these areas where such structures are temporary and often abandoned and new ones constructed. In most communities, most structures are considered generally permanent and thus sustainable.

The forests of the Good Roots Project

As noted earlier, the *barangay* of Subec, Dampig, San Isidro, and Saliksik are situated between the lowlands of the South China Sea and the western foothills of the Cordillera Central, a distance of eight straight-line kilometers. The lowland Ilocano communities of Subec, Dampig, and San Isidro are farmed to paddy and dry plow cultivation. All of these *barangay*, however, have some hilly sections that are covered by secondary forest. In general, the area is farmed-over monsoon dipterocarp forest with considerable secondary forest growth in the foothills. The highest peak in the area is 1,200 meters although human occupation does not extend above the 418 meter mark. The area is characterized by a traditional monsoon climate with pronounced rainy and dry seasons. The Ilocano settlements in this area were not firmly established until the middle to latter part of the nineteenth century but since then have evolved into what may be termed "typical" Ilocos Norte communities. The Yapayao community of Saliksik is upland. According to informants and an examination of their estimated birth dates, the Yapayao have been practicing *kaingin* cultivation in Saliksik for at least a hundred years and have been in the general area much longer. Presently, all *kaingin* activity in the area is carried out in secondary forest growth although two *kaingin*s are within a few meters of primary growth.

Based on a detailed survey by the Good Roots research team, the tree species characterizing the primary forest and secondary forest of the area are detailed in accompanying tables. There is, of course, a greater diversity of species in a secondary forest than in a primary forest.

An analysis of the ten sample plots measuring 10 meter by 10 meter shows that the total volume of trees with a diameter of 50 centimeters or above at breast height in the primary forest is 60.06654 cubic meters per 1,000 square meters or 600.6654 cubic meters per hectare. The total volume of trees between 2 centimeters and 49 centimeters is 25.774088 cubic meters per 1,000 square meters. The total volume of wood (trees) in the primary forest per 1,000 square meters is 85.840628 cubic meters or 858.40628 cubic meters per hectare.

Expressed in numbers of trees in a primary forest (Table 4.1), there are seven quality timber trees with a diameter of 50 centimeters or more per 1,000 square meters. There are 112 timber trees between 2 centimeters and 49 centimeters per 1,000 square meters. There are 156 trees of non-commercial quality (but useful) between 2 centimeters and 49 centimeters per 1,000 square meters. This means that in a primary forest in the Good Roots area the total number of trees per 1,000 square meters is 275 or there are 2,750 trees per hectare.

There are no trees in the secondary growth forest (Table 4.2) in the Good Roots area that exceed 50 centimeters in diameter at breast height. An analysis of the three sample plots 10 meters by 10 meters reveals that there are 14.01366 cubic meters per hectare of timber quality trees above 2 centimeters in diameter in the area. There are 77.308466 cubic meters per hectare of fuelwood species and 7.46760 cubic meters per hectare of minor construction species. In total, the volume of trees

Table 4.1 Common tree species in the primary forest

Common name	Ilocano name	Scienfitic name
Kalolot	*Obien*	*Artocarpus rubrovenius*
Katong matsing	*Baaken*	*Chrisocheton pentandrus*
Bayok	*Talingan*	*Pterospermum diversifolium*
Batino	*Panganoladsiem*	*Alstonia macrophylla*
Tibig	*Tebbeg*	*Ficus nota*
Panglomboien	*Pangleongboyen*	*Syzygium simile*
Taingang babui	*Taingang babui*	*Gonocaryum calleryanum*
Danupra	*Danupra*	*Toona sureni*
Malatibig	*Maratebbeg*	*Ficus congesta*
Amigis	*Amugis*	*Koordersiodendro pinnatum*
Tanguile	*Tanguili*	*Shorea polysperma*
Sablot	*Sablot*	*Litsea sebifera*
White lauan	*Apnit*	*Shorea contorta*
Apitong	*Apitong*	*Dipterocarpus grandiflorus*
Pildes	*Pildes*	*Garcinia dives*
Sakat	*Sakat*	*Terminalia nitens*
Patangis	*Patangis*	*Talauma villeriana*
Mayapis	*Mayapis*	*Shorea squamata*
Paitan	*Paitan*	*Cleidon javanicum*
Dalunot	*Dalunot*	*Pipturus arborescens*
Binggas	*Binggas*	*Terminalia citrina*
Luktob	*Kadir*	*Duabanga moluccana*
Paguringon	*Sarimbaboy*	*Cratoxylum sumatranum*
Malakmalak	*Banglas*	*Palaquium philippense*
Kalubkob	*Kalubkob*	*Syzygium caluncob*
Guijo	*Pisek*	*Shorea guiso*
Malapapaya	*Marapapaya*	*Polyscias nodosa*
Agusip	*Arusip*	*Symplocos ahernii*
Bitanghol	*Pamittaogen*	*Callophyllum blancoi*
Yakal	*Seggay*	*Shorea astylosa*
Katmon	*Palali*	*Dillenia philippinensis*
Lipang kalabaw	*Alupat nauang*	*Dendrocnicle meyeniana*
Igio	*Igio*	*Dysoxylum arborescens*
Mamalis	*Alumamani*	*Pittosporum pentandrum*
Danglin	*Alinao*	*Grewia multiflora*
Kalumpit	*Kalupit*	*Terminalia microcarpa*

Table 4.2 Common tree species in the secondary forest

Common name	Ilocano name	Scienfitic name
Lagundi	*Dangla*	*Vitex negundo*
Katong matsing	*Baaken*	*Chisocheton pentandrus*
Pahutan	*Pao*	*Mangifera altisima*
Guava	*Bayabas*	*Psidium gaujava*
Balinghasai	*Balinghasai*	*Buchanania arborescens*
Binunga	*Samak*	*Macaranga tanarius*
Takip asin	*Labuyok*	*Macaranga grandifolia*
Hamindang	*Bago*	*Macaranga bicolor*
Anabiong	*Agandong*	*Trema orientalis*
Antipolo	*Pakak bakir*	*Artocarpus blancoi*
Nangka	*Anangka*	*Artocarpus heterophyllus*
Anubing	*Anubing*	*Artocarpus ovatus*
Kalulot	*Kalolot*	*Artocarpus rubrovenius*
Himbabao	*Allokon*	*Broussonetia luzunica*
Aplas	*Aplas*	*Ficus congesta*
Bibig	*Tebbeg*	*Ficus nota*
Niog-niogan	*Basar-basar*	*Ficus pseodopalma*
Hauili	*Rayya-rayya*	*Ficus septica*
Is-is	*Aplis*	*Ficus ulmifolia*
Tangisang bayawak	*Latabak*	*Ficus variegata*
Kalios	*Aludig*	*Streblus asper*
Lipang kalabaw	*Alupat nuang*	*Dendrocnicle meyeniana*
Dalunot	*Mara sablot*	*Pinturus arborescens*
Patangis	*Patangis*	*Talauma villarrina*
Anonas	*Anonang*	*Annona reticulata*
Berbiba	*Beriba*	*Rollinia mucosa*
Sablot	*Sablot*	*Litsea sebifera*
Avacado	*Avacado*	*Persea gratissima*
Ipil	*Ipil*	*Intsia bijuga*
Dapdap	*Salbang*	*Erythrima orientalis*
Kakawate	*Madre*	*Gliricidia sepium*
Narra	*Dungon*	*Pterocarpus indicus*
Akleng parang	*Adaan*	*Albizia procera*
Salingkugi	*Maratekka*	*Albizia saponaria*
Ipil-ipil	*Komitis*	*Leucana leococephala*
Camachile	*Damortis*	*Pitchecellobium dulce*
Rain tree	*Algarrobo*	*Samanea saman*
Kabuyaw	*Kaburaw*	*Citrus macropterra*
Lukban	*Dugmon*	*Citrus grandis*
Pangsahingin	*Anteng*	*Canarium asperum*
Igyo	*Igyo*	*Dysoxylum decandrum*
Danupra	*Danupra*	*Toona sureni*
Bignai	*Bugnay*	*Antisdesma bunius*
Binai pugo	*Arosip*	*Antisdesma pentandrum*
Paitan	*Paitan*	*Cleidion javanicum*
Alim	*Alem*	*Mallotus multiglandulosus*
Tuai	*Duweg*	*Bischofia javanica*
Dao	*Makadeg*	*Dracontomelon dao*

Table 4.2 Continued

Common name	Ilocano name	Scienfitic name
Kamiring	Kamiring	Semecarpus philippinensis
Uas	Uas	Harpulia arborea
Kusibeng	Kusibeng	Sapindus saponaria
Malugai	Malugai	Pometia pinnata
Amamali	Amamali	Leea aculata
Danglin	Alinao	Grewia multiflora
Tan-ag	Butnong	Kleinhovia hospita
Bayok-bayokan	Baroy	Pterospermum cebicum
Kalumpang	Bangar	Sterculia foetida
Bitanghol	Pamittaogen	Callophyllum blancoi
Bitaog	Bitaog	Callophyllum inophyllum
Paguringun	Paguringun	Cratoxylum sumatranum
Tanguile	Tangili	Shorea polysperma
Luktob	Kadir	Duabanga moluccana
Kalumpit	Kalupit	Terminalia microcarpa
Sakat	Sakat	Terminalia nitens
Kalubkob	Kalubkob	Syzygium calubcob
Duhat	Lumboy	Syzygium cumini
Panglomboien	Panglongboien	Syzygium simile
Malapapaya	Marapapaya	Polyscias nodosa
Philippine ash	Suit	Fraximus griffithii
Batino	Panganuladsien	Alstonia macrophylla
Dita	Dalipaweng	Alstonia scholaris
Laneta	Lanuti	Wrightia pubescens
Lipang aso	Alupa	Lapptea spp.
Alagaw	Agraw	Premna odorata blanco
Lingo-lingo	Lingo-lingo	Viticipremna philippinenis
Molave	Sagat	Vitex parviflora
Bangkal	Bulala	Nauclea orientalis
Nino	Apatot	Morinda bracteata
Malatabako	Maratabako	Elephantopus tomentosus
Yakal	Seggay	Shorea astylosa

found in a Good Roots secondary forest is 98.78913 cubic meters per hectare.

Translated into the number of trees in the secondary growth areas, there are 1,366 timber value trees, 3,500 fuelwood trees, and 333 minor construction value trees for a total of 5,199 trees per hectare. In addition, there are 13,799 wildlings per hectare, bringing the total number of trees per hectare in the secondary forest to 18,998.

A comparison of primary and secondary forest shows a dramatic difference in woods available for use or misuses by society. While there

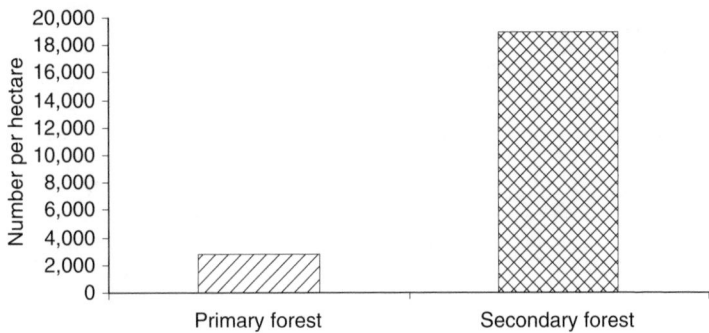

Figure 4.1 Trees in forest.

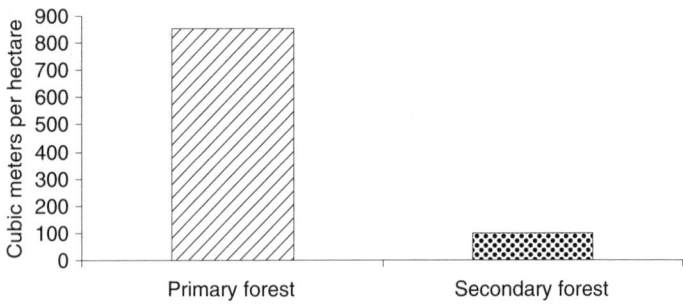

Figure 4.2 Volume: trees in forest.

are more trees per hectare in a secondary than a primary forest (18,998 as opposed to 2,750), in wood volume, there is far more wood in a primary forest (858.40628 as compared to 98.78913). When a primary forest is cleared and then allowed to develop to secondary growth, there is a reduction in wood volume of 760 cubic meters per hectare or 840 percent. Given this figure, an area of only 10 kilometers by 10 kilometers (10,000 hectares) the reduction would be 7,600,000 cubic meters of wood loss. The loss would be even greater if the primary forest was replaced by grass rather than by secondary tree growth. In the area under examination here, almost all tree loss in both primary and secondary forests has been caused and continues to be caused by human intervention (Figures 4.1 and 4.2).

Plate 1 The author with a Yapayao participant.

Plate 2 Ilocano boy helping in the nursery.

(Note: Photos courtesy of the author.)

Plate 3 A Good Roots participant receiving coconuts for her farm.

Plate 4 Young Good Roots participant presenting a seedling to the secretary of the DENR (Cover).

Plate 5 Transporting seedlings from the community nursery to her farm.

Plate 6 A Good Roots community nursery.

Plate 7 Giving credit to the financial donor.

Plate 8 Pulling illegal log from the forest to the lowlands.

Plate 9 Typical rural Ilocano church.

Plate 10 A common mode of travel.

Plate 11 House of a poor Ilocano family.

Plate 12 Collecting social census data.

Plate 13 A typical *kaingin.*

Plate 14 Yapayao giving speech at award ceremony.

Plate 15 Good Roots staff waiting for outcome of stewardship petition.

Plate 16 Planting paddy rice.

Plate 17 Installing rain gauge in *kaingin*.

Plate 18 Teaching is a daily Good Roots activity.

Plate 19 Pagudpud Town Hall.

Plate 20 Yapayao houses located in *kaingin*s.

Plate 21 Yapayao ritual specialist with sacrificial puppy.

5 Cultural exploitation of the forests

As noted, the people of Subec, Dampig, San Isidro and Saliksik affect their forest areas through *kaingin* cultivation, charcoal-making, fuelwood consumption, illegal logging and the cutting of trees for minor construction. While all of these *barangay* share in these cultural activities, the extent to which the forest is affected is community- and activity-specific. For example, all of the households in Saliksik practice *kaingin* cultivation while in San Isidro only 17 of the 108 households practice *kaingin* farming. Charcoal-making is not an activity in all of the communities. Illegal logging is not important in all of the villages. An appreciation for these human–nature relationships as expressed in the ways cultural practices contribute to deforestation requires an understanding of the specifics of the human intervention into nature.

Kaingin cultivation

Slash-and-burn or shifting cultivation by both the Yapayao and Ilocano in the study areas fundamentally conform to slash-and-burn farming as practiced in other parts of Southeast Asia. All the households in Saliksik (35) cultivate a total of 50 *kaingin*s. In Subec there are 21 *kaingin*s, 39 in Dampig and 17 in San Isidro. Saliksik has the largest average size *kaingin* (0.3452 hectares) while the smallest average size *kaingin* is in Dampig (0.0616 hectares). In Saliksik *kaingin* farming is the primary source of income while in the Ilocano communities, *kaingin* activity is secondary to lowland paddy and dry field plow farming. The Yapayao are the most environmentally considerate *kaingin* cultivators and attempt to protect their lands by farming an area for only one year (two cropping seasons) and then allow the *kaingin* to lie fallow for 4–5 years before farming it again. Some of the Ilocano *kaingin* farmers follow the *kaingin* practices of the Yapayao while others over cultivate the land by farming an area for several years in succession. As noted, presently all *kaingin* activity in the area is in secondary forest growth areas.

For purposes of analysis, the *kaingin*s in Dampig should be separated from the *kaingin*s in the other communities, not because of techniques but because of the characteristics of the growth in which the *kaingin*s are worked. The *kaingin*s in Saliksik, Subec, and San Isidro are cut from typical secondary forest with a high plant diversity index and a total of 18,998 trees per hectare. The *kaingin*s in Dampig are cut from artificially established secondary growth that produced 18,266 trees per hectare (above and below 2 centimeters in diameter), most of which are the species *Leucaena leococephala* (*ipil-ipil*). This species, primarily used as fuelwood, was established in Dampig in 1982–1983. In Subec, San Isidro, and Saliksik, the volume of trees in cubic meters is 98.78911 per hectare. In Dampig, there are 94.07033 cubic meters per hectare.

In terms of trees lost/cut to *kaingin* cultivation, the people in Saliksik farm 50 *kaingin*s with an average size of 3,452 square meters for a total of 17.26 hectares. In Subec, there are 21 *kaingin*s with an average size of 800 square meters for a total of 1.68 hectares. There are 17 *kaingin*s in San Isidro with an average size of 1,352 square meters with a total of 2.3 hectares. The people of Dampig farm to *kaingin* a total of 2.4 hectares in 39 *kaingin*s with an average size of 615 square meters.

Given the data on forests and *kaingin*s, this means that in Saliksik, almost 328,000 trees are lost to *kaingin* activity each year; almost 32,000 trees are cut for *kaingin* each year in San Isidro; in Subec, around 43,000 trees are lost; and in Dampig, around 44,000 trees are cut for *kaingin* each year. In total, the four Good Roots communities cut 447,000 trees of secondary forest on 23.64 hectares each year in order to maintain their *kaingin* activity.

Charcoal-making

Charcoal-making is not a significant activity among Good Roots villagers although it does account for some tree loss in the area. Presently, there are only eleven households, all in San Isidro, making charcoal, most of which is for home consumption. Five households in other *barangay* have recently stopped making charcoal because of the difficulty of obtaining the needed wood.

Charcoal in the area is made via what is generally called the "pit method." This involves first digging a hole in the ground sufficiently large to accommodate the desired volume of wood. In general, the pit is 40–50 centimeters deep and 150 by 150 centimeters wide. A bed of dried leaves is established in the pit, followed by placement of the logs to be turned into charcoal, the smaller pieces placed on the bottom. The pit is then filled with rice chaff and mounded to about one foot above the ground. The rice chaff is lighted and the smoldering fire turns the logs to charcoal in two to four days depending on the size of the logs and whether they are dried or freshly cut.

Testing the maturity of the charcoal is done by two methods. In the first test, a pointed stick is pushed to the bottom of the pit and an experienced charcoal maker recognizes whether or not to remove the charcoal. Taking the charcoal from the pit prematurely renders the charcoal inferior; waiting too long to remove the charcoal causes the wood stock to turn to ash. The other test is to dig into the pit and examine the state of the wood. Regardless of the test used, when the charcoal is taken from the pit, it is submerged in water and then sun dried for a few days.

Charcoal-makers prefer the harder wood species such as *narra* (*Pterocarpus indicus*), *bitaog* (*Callophyllum inophyllum*), *camachile* (*Pithecellobium dulce*), and *kakawate* (*Gliricidia sepium*) ranging in size from 10 to 120 meters in diameter. In San Isidro, because of the availability in nearby forests, the predominant species used in charcoal-making is *camachile*.

Determining the actual number of trees lost to charcoal-making in the area is difficult because of the various ways wood is secured. In some cases, wood is scavenged from riverbanks and forests, in others it is obtained by using the by-products of illegal logging, and in others, by actually cutting trees. Charcoal-makers and researchers estimate that approximately 50 percent of the wood for charcoal-making comes from gathering and the other 50 percent comes from the cutting of trees.

In San Isidro, the charcoal-making households, by actual measurement of a 30 percent sample, use an average of 0.1875 cans (0.0625 cubic meters) or 0.01172 cubic meters of charcoal per day. The average volume of a *camachile* tree, the common tree cut for charcoal, is 0.75155 cubic meters or it produces 12,0248 cans of charcoal. As each household consumes 0.01172 cubic meters of charcoal per day, each household consumes 4.2778 cubic meters of charcoal per year. This means that each household uses 5.69179 *camachile* trees per year or the 11 charcoal-making households consume a total of 62.61167 trees per year.

In reality, however, because only 50 percent of the wood used in charcoal making comes directly from cutting trees, the number of trees lost in San Isidro each year, mainly from secondary forest growth, is only 31.30583.

Fuelwood consumption

As noted in detail elsewhere (Wallace 1995b), fuelwood consumption is a significant contributor to tree loss in the four Good Roots communities. Importantly, however, the use or loss of trees to fuelwood is not a sign of environmental disregard on the part of the farmers, it is a function of other sources of fuel being unavailable or too expensive.

By farmer preference and availability, the most common species of tree used as fuelwood by the four communities, all coming from secondary growth areas, are *ipil-ipil* (*Leucaena leucocephala*), *binunga* (*Macaranga tanarius*), *lagundi* (*Vitex negundo*), *camachile* (*Pitchecellabium dulce*), *kakawate* (*Gliricidian sepium*), and *suit* (*Fraximus griffithii*). These species are fast growing and relatively small with a main trunk ranging in diameter from 4.5 to 11 centimeters with branches ranging from 1.5 to 4.5 centimeters in diameter. In general, the species have a low volume of wood. For example, an *ipil-ipil* tree at 2–3 years' maturity provides only 0.014 cubic meters of fuelwood. At 4–5 years, a suit tree is 10 meters tall but has a main trunk of 4.0–5.0 centimeters in diameter and provides only 0.009 cubic meters of fuelwood. The men tend to cut trees for fuelwood and men, women or children carry it back to the village. While there is some variation in fuelwood consumption because of seasonal temperatures and special celebrations, on average, the variation is not significant.

Based on 1992 population figures, an average of all species of fuelwood consumed by household per day in the four study villages is, as follows: Subec, 0.022 cubic meters; Dampig, 0.030 cubic meters; San Isidro, 0.020 cubic meters; and Saliksik, 0.019 cubic meters. This means that the people in Subec consume 1,801 cubic meters of fuelwood per year; in Dampig they consume 1,467 cubic meters per year; in San Isidro, 848 cubic meters per year; and in Saliksik, 194 cubic meters of fuelwood per year. The variance here is primarily a function of population size.

Converted to tree equivalency, the people of Subec use as fuelwood 57.1 trees per person per year; in Dampig, each person consumes 49.2 trees per year; in San Isidro, each person consumes 60 trees per year; and in Saliksik, each man, woman and child consumes 105.7 trees per year for fuelwood. The significant difference in number of trees consumed per person between the lowland Ilocano communities and the upland Yapayao is primarily a function of the fact that the trees are smaller, they are more readily available in Saliksik and there is a greater need for fuelwood because of a longer cold season.

In terms of the 1993–1994 population in the study villages, the people of Subec consume more than 236,000 of the small fuelwood tree species per year; Dampig consumes a total of 38,000 trees per year as fuelwood; in San Isidro, the residents consume more than 59,000 trees as fuelwood per year; and in Saliksik, the people consume around 18,500 trees per year. In total, the four Good Roots communities consume more than 352,000 fuelwood trees each year.

Illegal logging

Except with governmental approval, the cutting of hardwood trees is prohibited in the Philippines. There are numerous laws governing this activity but because of a lack of monitoring power and the corruption of some local officials, illegal logging is a significant enterprise in the country. In the northwestern part of Ilocos Norte there are no large illegal logging operations. There are, however, many small-scale independent illegal logging farmers. In the Good Roots communities there are 15 illegal logging teams, each team composed of 4–7 men. Because of the sensitive nature of collecting the data on this activity, the villages where these teams are based are referred to here as Village I, Village II, and Village III. Village I has four teams, Village II has two teams, and Village III has nine teams. The basic tools of illegal logging in the area are chain saws, axes, machetes, and digging bars.

Logging by these teams is done in primary forest growth areas, usually 3–4 hours walking from the home village. The most common species being cut by the illegal loggers are *narra* (*Pterocarpus indicus*), *tanguile* (*Shorea polysperma*), *apnit* (*Shorea contorta*), *guijo* (*Shorea guiso*), *yakal* (*Shorea astylosa*), *almaciga* (*Agathis philippinesis*), and *dao* (*Dracentomelon dao*). These are usually large trees, often reaching a full height of 20 meters with a diameter of 1 meter.

Each logging team consists of a main chain-saw operator, an assistant operator and two, perhaps three, companions. The team usually goes into the forest with the intention of staying there for 3–5 days. The number of logging trips they make each year depends on the current demand and price of illegally cut wood. Most of the loggers maintain a reserve stock of felled trees in the forest in order to avoid detection by authorities and to insure a supply of wood on demand from buyers. Loggers say that freshly cut logs are too heavy to transport out of the forest and that logs are best seasoned in the forest.

The responsibilities of the chain-saw operator and his assistant are to decide the direction of the fall, decide on the size of the squared logs to be cut from the felled trees, care of the chainsaw and make all major sawing cuts. The companions are responsible for cleaning the surroundings of the cutting area, cutting and preparing trees as scaffolding in case the buttress is too high or cutting at the basal of the tree is not possible, overseeing the routing of log transportation, and moving the logs away from the cutting site.

Transportation of the logs, generally cut into what are called squared logs (usually 25 centimeters by 30 centimeters by 4 meters), are pulled from the forest by *carabao* (water buffalo) or by what is called the "balloon method" (where the logs are supported by inflated automobile inner-tubes and floated down river).

The buyers and end-users of the illegal logs are usually outside the *barangay*. Depending on the buyer, the logs are purchased as logs, squared logs, or as sized lumber.

Data from general interviews with villagers and loggers, detailed interviews with logging team leaders, visits to logging sites, and the actual measurement of trees and cut logs in three logging sites, suggest that although illegal logging in the Good Roots villages is small-scale, it is a significant activity. The total volume of major timber trees cut by the four teams in Village I is 120.46 cubic meters per year. The two teams in Village II cut 60.22 cubic meters per year of timber trees. Village III, with nine teams, cut a total of 271.03 cubic meters of timber trees per year. In addition, smaller timber and lesser value trees are cut or destroyed in preparing the site and when associated with timber-cutting. Village I cuts 8.28 cubic meters of smaller trees per year. Village II destroys 4.14 cubic meters of lesser trees and Village III cuts 18.62 of these trees in association with timber activity.

Including saplings destroyed or seriously damaged in association with illegal logging activities, the people in Village I extract from the forest 183.33 trees each year; Village II loggers extract 91.68 trees from the forest; and the logging teams in Village III extract 412.50 trees from the forest. In total, the Good Roots communities extract 687.50 trees from nature through illegal logging activities each year, all from primary forest growth areas.

Minor construction

Although the construction of temporary houses and granaries in the *kaingin*s are a minor contributor to the loss of forest reserves in the Good Roots area, the activity is worth noting. The common species used (along with bamboo and thatching material) in the construction of temporary houses and granaries are *lagundi* (*Vitex negundo*), *baroy* (*Pterospesmum cebicum*), and *suit* (*Fraximus griffithii*). These small fuelwood-type trees thrive in secondary forest growth.

Based on measurements of temporary houses and granaries, the average volume of wood used in the construction of one of these structures is 0.23 cubic meters. As there are 30 temporary houses and 13 granaries in the *kaingin*s, the total volume of wood used in this construction is 9.80 cubic meters. Expressed in terms of trees extracted from the forest, 60.75 of these trees are cut in order to construct one of these structures. For the whole of the Good Roots communities, a total of around 260 trees are used each year in the construction of *kaingin* structures.

The uses and misuses of trees by human populations are an expressive indicator of the delicate relationships between culture and nature. The data from the Good Roots communities are illustrative of the limitations of nature and the impact of culture on nature. But not all lost trees are an equal loss to the environment. The cutting of a single hardwood tree in primary forest growth is a greater loss than the cutting of a fuelwood tree in secondary forest growth; most fuelwood trees, because they are abundant and fast growing, will regenerate in only a few years whereas the loss of a hardwood tree may be a loss forever (Figures 5.1 and 5.2). This becomes even more important considering that there are 858 cubic meters per hectare of wood in trees in primary forest growth while there are only 98 cubic meters per hectare in secondary forest growth even though there are 18,998 trees per hectare in secondary forest areas and only 2,750 trees per hectare in primary growth areas.

The data from the Good Roots Project presented here demonstrate that even though charcoal-making can be an environmentally

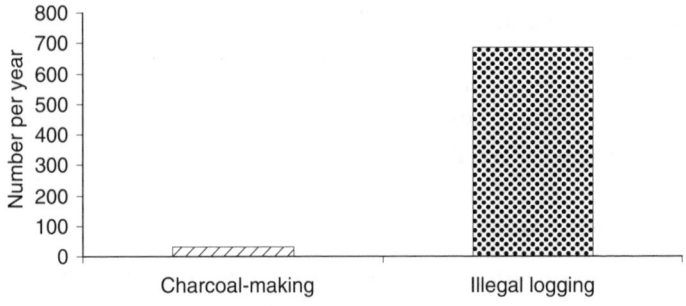

Figure 5.1 Tree lost: primary forest.

Figure 5.2 Trees and wildlings lost: secondary forest.

destructive activity, it is relatively unimportant in the study villages. Likewise, the loss of trees because of minor construction also is relatively unimportant. Charcoal-making is insignificant mainly because only 11 of the 473 Good Roots households are making charcoal. Although each charcoal-making household uses only 5 trees per year, if the 11 households increased to 20 or 50 households, then there would be a serious impact on the environment. Because the temporary houses and granaries in the *kaingin*s are made from small secondary growth trees and there are few of these structures, it is unlikely that minor construction activity will become a significant contributor to tree loss in the near future.

The significant cultural contributors to tree loss in the Good Roots area are *kaingin* cultivation, fuelwood consumption and illegal logging. It is in these arenas where culture has the most dramatic impact on nature. Between *kaingin* cultivation and fuelwood use, the four communities consume a total of 800,000 trees per year or a total of 42 hectares of trees each year. This means that every man, woman and child on an average consume 290 trees each year or 1.53 percent of a hectare of secondary growth forest each year. The only positive side of this figure comes from the observation that given the cultural practices in the area associated with *kaingin* farming and fuelwood consumption, most of this deforested land should return to secondary growth. If grasses, particularly *cogon* or *Imperata cylindrica*, were a serious problem as is the case on the eastern slopes of the Cordillera Central (around the Cagayan Valley) or further south on the western slopes, such a loss could be an environmental disaster.

Illegal logging presents a different type of problem because all of the felled trees are from primary forest growth. The only cultural explanation of the persistence of this illegal practice is simple greed; the farmer-loggers are no poorer than the other residents of the area. Presently, only 687 hardwood trees or 0.25 trees per person are extracted each year by the Good Roots communities. This constitutes 24 percent of a hectare of primary growth forest. If the 15 teams of illegal loggers increased to 60, for example, then almost one hectare of non-replaceable timber would be lost each year. This would be a regrettable but environmentally tolerable situation if only the four Good Roots communities were involved in illegal logging. But these communities constitute only 34 percent of the population of the *barangay* in the immediate vicinity and other *barangay* also have illegal logging teams.

If tree loss by humans is projected to include the adjacent six *barangay*, there is a loss of 2,349,000 trees or 123 hectares of secondary growth forest in the area each year (including the loss from the Good Roots *barangay*). In primary forest growth, projections for the Good Roots and nearby *barangay* are 2,025 trees per year or 0.73 hectares. It should be remembered, however, that there is almost nine times the volume of wood in the primary forest as there is in the secondary forest. Given this situation, illegal logging is having a significant impact on the local environment.

If population growth in the Good Roots region is comparable to the national average of the Philippines, the population in the area will double over the next two to three decades creating even greater demands from the environment. Under this situation, it is only a matter of time, less than a generation, before the forests of the area are almost fully denuded. As the human–nature relationships stand today, considering the unlikelihood that alternatives to fuelwood use and *kaingin* cultivation will become available and that curtailment of illegal logging will be forthcoming, the environmental situation will worsen in the future. Given this scenario, it seems reasonable, although regrettable, to accept the reality of the pending environmental calamity and develop a strategy to reclaim the forests as they are being denuded. The farmer-participants in the Good Roots agriculture and forestry development project are attempting to accomplish this end— they are working to reclaim their upland environment and bring stability to culture–nature relationships in the area.

6 Good Roots development

Introduction

The data is clear that humanity, through social and technological practices, is responsible for the imminent environmental calamity facing the Philippines and other Southeast Asian countries. As humanity is a major contributor to these violations of nature, then it also falls to humanity to try to repair the damage that has already been done. The role of Good Roots is to assist farm families in going about the business of reclaiming their environment.

At the start of the project, the initial step was to identify both formal and informal leadership in the communities. This allowed the team immediate access to the community and led to a better implementation of the project. The formal leaders were members of the *barangay* council. The informal leaders, identified after the research team had established good rapport in the area, were men and women who were respected because of their work habits and insights and officers in such community organizations as the mother's clubs, youth clubs, and other voluntary associations. Some of these acknowledged leaders, of course, were more effective spokespersons for Good Roots than others. The purpose of Good Roots was explained to these leaders and as the team began to conduct basic socioeconomic surveys, the results of the surveys were shared with the leaders and other community members. Building rapport in the research and development communities was greatly eased because the team members were all Ilocano speakers.

After the initial RRA was completed, numerous formal meetings were held in each of the four Good Roots *barangay*. These early meetings were to inform the public and to motivate people to participate in Good Roots. Thereafter, quarterly meetings were held in all the *barangay*. In time, as the farmers increasingly gained confidence in

Good Roots, these meetings were reduced. Numerous informal meetings continued to be held with the community, associations, and individuals.

Nurseries

A structural underpinning of Good Roots is the office nursery. It sets the standard for the Good Roots nurseries located in the villages and provides for the research and development team an accessible place to conduct germination and seedling experiments. This 315 square meters plot allows participants to actively plan their own future rather than having to react to instructions from some authorative development group. Most of the tree seeds were collected locally but some were sourced in Manila, Los Baños, Aparri, and elsewhere. If farmers expressed a preference for a particular tree species, every effort was made to obtain seeds for germination. The office nursery area, located adjacent to the house/office, serves as the primary place for the production of buffer seedlings stocks, a place where species may be germinated, and an area where intensive care and maintenance experiments may be conducted. The house nursery, including a small greenhouse, is protected by a fence from animals and human traffic. This nursery is located on land that was previously nonproductive.

Operating the office nursery is a time-consuming and labor-intensive activity revolving around seed production and seedling maintenance.

Since the beginning of the project, excluding numerous species of vegetable seeds, forty-two different tree species have been collected for the purpose of seedling production. Deciding on the species to procure reflects a cooperative effort on the part of Good Roots and the local farmers. There are certain tree species, many of them local, which the research team decided to develop. In addition, local farmers were systematically surveyed as to which species they wanted as a part of the Good Roots Project. Drawing farmers into the decision-making process proved to be a very positive activity; they were given the opportunity to plan their own future rather than having to react to "experts" representing the authority of a development group.

The early growth or pre-emergence period of seeds varies from one species to another. Some seeds germinate fast while other take considerably more time. In some cases, it is necessary to carry out seed treatment processes such as cracking the nut, chopping the husk or removal of the seed coat in order to facilitate emergence. Some of the larger seeds are sown directly to polyethylene bags or pots (ranging in size from $4'' \times 6''$ to $5''$ by $7''$ to $6'' \times 9''$) and then placed in pot beds constructed from bamboo. Smaller seeds are sown directly in seed boxes located in the greenhouse to germinate before they are pricked and planted in polyethylene bags and placed in pot beds. The fastest maturing Good Roots species is eucalyptus, which takes only fifteen days from sowing before it is ready for pricking. The slowest of the species are palms such as betel nut and *anahaw*, which may take up to two months before they can be pricked and planted in pots (see Table 6.1).

Table 6.1 Most common Good Roots species

Common name	Ilocano name	Scientific name
Forest species		
Big leaf mahogany	*mahogani*	*Switenia macrophylla*
Narra	*dungon*	*Pterocarpus indicus*
Tanguile	*tanguile*	*Shoria polysperma*
Philippine ash	*suit*	*Fraximus griffithii*
Rain tree	*algarrobo*	*Samaea saman*
Acacia	*auri*	*Acacia auriculiformis*
Eucalyptus	*eucalyptus*	*Eucalyptus camaldullensis*
Palomaria	*bitaog*	*Calophyllum inophyllum*
Ipil-ipil	*komkompitis*	*Leucaena leucocephala*
Fruit species		
Calamansi	*kalamamsi*	*Citrus microcarpa*
Mango	*mangga*	*Magifera indica*
Pomelo	*dogmon*	*Citrus grandis*
Hamlin	*kahel*	*Citrus aurantium*
American lemon	*lemon*	*Citrus sp.*
Cashew	*kasoy*	*Anacardium occidentale*
Jackfruit	*anangka*	*Artucarpus hetrophyllus*
Soursop	*gayobano*	*Annana auricata*
Sugar apple	*atis*	*Annona squamosa*
Santol	*santol*	*Sandoricum koetjape*
Breadfruit	*pakak*	*Artucarpus communis*
Coffee	*kape*	*Coffea robusta*
Papaya	*papaya*	*Carica papaya*
Rambutan	*rambutan*	*Nephelium lappaceum*
Lansones	*lansones*	*Lansium domesticum*
Balobo	*bagobo*	*Diplodiscus pandiculatus*
Cacao	*kakaw*	*Theobroma cacao*
Kapok	*kapas*	*Ceiba pentandra*
Avocado	*abokado*	*Persea americana*
Tamarind	*salamagi*	*Tamarindus indica*
Passion fruit	*grandilla*	*Passiflora edulis*
Guava	*guapol*	*Psidium guajava*
Pineapple	*pinya*	*Anonas comosos*
Iba	*karmay*	*Averhoa sp.*
Orange (var.)	*sibat*	*Citrus sp.*
Mandarin	*mandarin*	*Citrus sp.*
Orange (var.)	*ladu*	*Citrus sp.*

(*Table 6.1 continued*)

Table 6.1 Continued

Common name	Ilocano name	Scientific name
Palm and Pandan		
Pandan	*sarakat*	*Pandanus* sp.
Anahaw	*labig*	*Livistona rotundifolia*
Betelnut	*bua*	*Areca catechu*
Coconut	*niog*	*Cocos nucifera*
Vegetables		
Pegion pea	*kardis*	*Cajanus canan*
Eggplant	*tarong*	*Solanum melongena*
Tomato	*kamatis*	*Lycopersicon esculentum*
Okra	*okra*	*Hibiscus esculentus*
Sweet pepper	*sili*	*Capsicum annuum*
Bittergourd	*parya*	*Momordica charantia*
Stringbeans	*sitaw*	*Vigna sesquipedalis*
Luffa	*tabau-tabua*	*Luffa cylindrica*
Squash	*karabasa*	*Cucurbita maxima*

Most common Good Roots species

To enhance growth and insure a healthy plant after the seeds germinate are planted or pricked in polyethylene pots, considerable time is devoted to weeding. This lessens competition for the available nutrients in the potted soil and minimizes the possibility of harmful insects. Inorganic and foliar fertilizers are applied during the seedling maturation process. The pots are regularly cultivated to promote aeration and fungicides and insecticides are sprayed on the plants at least twice a month. If roots penetrate the plastic pots before it is time to plant the seedlings in the field, they are pruned to avoid field-planting shock, to promote new root growth, and enhance nutrient uptake. Topping is also carried out, especially in overgrown seedlings, to allow for a better rate of transpiration and absorption. The seedlings are watered daily before the time they are ready to be moved to a different potting bed.

Once the seedlings have reached a height of 25–30 centimeters, they are almost ready for planting in the field so they are re-stocked in a different pot bed for hardening. Hardening is an important step because it reduces transplanting shock during field planting. This is done by exposing the seedlings to more sunlight and decreasing their water supply. Without the hardening process, the seedlings would be subject to shock when they are transplanted in the fields.

Within a year of the start of Good Roots, the office nursery was operational and five communal nurseries had been established; one in Subec, Saliksik, and San Isidro and two in Dampig. Good Roots provides education, plastic bags, some insecticides and fertilizers, and an assortment of tools such as a sprayer, rake, spade, wheelbarrow, and other farming implements. The community participants contribute labor, indigenous materials used in construction and maintenance, and potting soil. The lands on which the nurseries are located are freely contributed by the community participants.

Because Good Roots is a FSR/D project in agroforestry, farmer-participants are not paid for their labor. The philosophy of Good Roots is one based on the premise that farmers who actively contribute to their own welfare will take their responsibilities seriously and rapidly move in the direction of self-determination. A "give-a-way" program will last only so long as there is a "give-a-way." Good Roots is a program promoting environmental education through individual and community participation. The Good Roots participants reap the reward of their own labors. Participants are "paid" with the seedlings they produce. The number of seedlings they receive is based on the number of hours they work in their nurseries.

While men, women and children all work in the nurseries, women are the most active laborers. Each participant family is required to contribute labor to the maintenance of the nursery. If the man of the household is unavailable for work, he sends his representative, usually his wife or occasionally an older child. Men tend to be most visible and outspoken at formal meetings while women tend to do most of the work in the nurseries. Women say they like to work in the nurseries because it is time they can set aside to visit with their neighbors. Men generally explain their occasional absence from work in the nursery by pointing out the demands of their farm. Transplantation of the seedlings nurtured in the nurseries to the field is shared equally by men and women.

Establishing nurseries in the Good Roots *barangay* has proved to be a key element in the success of the project. Having a nursery in the community exposes the participants to the risks and successes of seedling production. It is here, alongside their neighbors, they learn how to germinate and develop seedlings. Participants have a personal investment in the nursery and they take pride in their successes and commiserate with one another when a typhoon or other calamity destroys the nursery. A healthy competitive spirit is developed between different nurseries. Based on what they have learnt in the nursery, some participants have taken it upon themselves to collect local seeds and develop their own seedlings. The nurseries are a comfortable place for the Good Roots staff to work side by side with participants and to gather information about problems and determine the current views and concerns of the participants. In addition, the Good Roots staff frequently gives lectures at the nursery (as well in more formal meetings) on topics such as seedling production, care, and maintenance of seedlings, and pest and disease control. Finally, as the nurseries are located near the center of the villages, they attract the attention of non-participants and encourage participation.

Good Roots Associations and education

A "Good Roots Association" exists in each of the research and development communities of Subec, Dampig, San Isidro, and Saliksik. These associations were established at the suggestion of the Good Roots research team as a means of effective implementation and organization, as an environmental educational tool, to build a group identity, and as a way to promote environmental awareness. The formulation and establishment of these associations, however, was carried out by the Good Roots participants. Each Good Roots Association has its own elected set of officers (President, Vice President, Secretary/Treasurer, and Auditor and Press Information Officer). Through regularly scheduled meetings and work activities, these voluntary associations are in charge of overseeing all Good Roots activities in the communities. Good Roots staff members work with these associations in planning special educational trips, award ceremonies, and in addressing the inevitable problems associated with community development.

In addition to the daily work done with individual farmers and in the *barangay* nurseries, staff members meet formally each month with each Good Roots Association. During these meetings, staff members update the participants on the status of the project and inform them of program targets and upcoming events. In addition, the monthly meetings give participants an opportunity to share their experiences with other participants, welcome new members, discuss their successes and failures with the seedlings they have planted in their own farm areas, and to voice their concerns about Good Roots activities. If there are structural problems, they are expressed at these meetings. If the records show that the nursery is being neglected, for example, the membership is informed and a plan is made to rectify the situation. The intent of these meetings is to build an *esprit de corps* among the participants and to provide an open forum to discuss all matters pertaining to Good Roots. While these meetings are usually positive in orientation and very important rapport building tools, occasionally, controversial issues arise. For example, a situation developed in 1993 at one of these formal meetings when the members of the association in one of the villages voted out its Good Roots Association officers and voted in new officers. This unusual but dramatic move is illustrative of the seriousness to which many Good Roots members take their responsibility of trying to reclaim their environment.

As noted, a cornerstone of the Good Roots Project is seedling production and tree planting. Purchasing large numbers of seedlings is prohibitively expensive for most farmers. Therefore, the Good Roots Project produces from seed most of its own seedling. This approach is not only inexpensive, it is an education for farmers that will last beyond a single generation and it builds on the principle "self-help." Once the seedlings have matured, they are distributed to Good Roots participants for planting in and around their homes and fields. The Good Roots staff works closely with farmers in planting and in monitoring the growth and health of the plants.

In 1992, the year following the establishment of the nurseries and completion of the social, economic, and environmental surveys of the area, a total slightly more than 23,000 seedlings were produced in the different Good Roots nurseries. In addition, 317 seedlings were transported from University of the Philippines, P. Los Baños to the research and development area. This stock of seedlings represented twenty different species, 78 percent of which were mahogany, coffee, guapple (an improved breed of guava), and jackfruit.

During the latter part of 1992, as the Good Roots staff and farmers began to transplant seedlings from the nurseries to the field, an evaluation of the species developed during the year was undertaken. Emphasis was placed on farmer-participant preferences and needs so nursery production in 1993 increased to 26,436 seedlings. The species most in demand by the farmers during 1993 were mahogany, pineapple suckers, cashew, betel nut, kapok, *anahaw*, mango, breadfruit, and papaya.

Because farmers in Ilocos Norte are reluctant to plant trees on land that is unsecured and because of the large number of seedlings produced and trees planted during 1992 and throughout 1993, Good Roots seedling production was reduced in 1994. Total seedling production this year was 15,170, 75 percent of which were mahogany, native or mandarin orange, and calamandarin. Calamandarin was in demand by farmers because it serves as an excellent rootstock for budding and is resistant to citrus diseases. Mahogany continued to be in demand for its use in communal tree farms and by farmers with wide vacant lots. The farmer-participants developed a strong interest in native orange after being taken on a field trip where they learned from specialists the planting and care of this species and of the high profitability of the species.

Of the 65,000 Good Roots seedlings produced during 1992 through 1994, 50 percent were mahogany, coffee, calamansi, calamandarin, and jackfruit (Table 6.2). Other common seedlings produced were species such as eucalyptus, guaple, and guayabano. Except for mahogany and eucalyptus, most of the energy of the Good Roots staff and farmers was given over to the production and planting of fruit trees. This pattern reflected a strategy on the part of the Good Roots team. Early in the project, the team realized that the farmers needed to be able to see some rewards for their labors in a relatively short period of time. Citrus trees reach their economic potential more rapidly than do most other trees. Without this incentive it would be difficult to persuade farmers to invest of their time and labor. The team focused on mahogany as an important forest tree because of the contributions it makes to stabilizing the environment and because culturally, farmers perceive mahogany to be an important species. Eucalyptus was emphasized as a forest tree because of its rapid growth rate and because farmers, even though it is new to the area, perceive of it as a tree which brings beauty to their community.

Good Roots activity has brought about an increase in the number of seedlings produced and distributed to the farmers from the 1993 high. Although species with direct economic potential are still in the greatest demand by farmers, the Good Roots effort is now focused on getting farmers to plant more forest trees and to increasing the number of farmers who participate in the Good Roots Project.

Although seedling production and trees planting is the foundation on which Good Roots is constructed, the activities of the project extend far beyond this dimension into numerous other aspects of the community. Good Roots is first and foremost a humanity–earth–plant project designed to help farmers help themselves. Importantly, however, successful agroforestry development involves much more than the technical aspects of technology transfer. Unless an equal amount of energy is devoted to education, to changing people's perspective of the environment, and to addressing sociocultural problems associated with environment degradation, the project will not be successful and the designated recipients of planned change will suffer.

Table 6.2 Good Roots seedling production

Species	1992	1993	1994	Total
Calamansi	2,813	975	33	3,821
Mahogany	5,227	3,166	4,265	12,658
Narra		1,106	30	1,136
Cashew		2,060	196	2,256
Anahaw		1,554	550	2,104
Eucalyptus	1,845	885		2,730
Coffee	5,864	1,175	421	7,460
Jackfruit	2,315	601	24	2,940
Guaple	2,140	120	1	2,261
Papaya	265	1,210	47	1,522
Paminta	68			68
Lansones	83	58	42	183
American Lemon	62	539	35	636
Avacado	51	42	1	94
Pomelo	28	375	159	562
Guayabano	1,692	27	93	1,812
Breadfruit		1,315	19	1,334
Atis	200	13		213
Mandarin	41	594	1,030	1,665
Betelnut	173	1,770	536	2,479
Mango	36	1,363	135	1,665
Rambutan		189	22	211
Calamandarin			6,255	6,255
Cacao		87	129	216
Kapok		1,707	536	2,243
Tanguile		716		716
Tamarind		73	58	131
Pandan		160	370	540
Pineapple sucker		2,860		2,860
Balobo	95	46	2	147
Coconut	133	366		499
Santol		60	36	96
Auri	31	83	6	120
Raintree		116	95	211
Pasion fruit	52	16		52
Philippine ash	120	742	22	884
Celery		7		7
Bitaog		123	44	167
Magium			2	2
Ipil-ipil		153		153
Himbabao			7	7

In order to expose as many villagers as possible to the activities of Good Roots and to promote ecologically sensitive farming techniques, demonstration plots have been established in the *barangay* of Subec, Dampig, and Saliksik. With the help of the farmers in these communities, lands were selected for the demonstration plots. In all three cases, the land was unused and unproductive. Initially, the Good Roots team mapped the land and presented a carefully planned sketch map to the participants outlining the ideal farming systems for sloping lands. Using a homemade "A" frame, the farmers were taught how to creature contours and select the plants for the demonstration farm. Good Roots contributed knowledge to the project. The farmers contributed labor to the project.

Fruit tree species were planted along the contour lines. The larger of the species were planted along the lower slopes so that other plants would not be too shaded as they matured. Pineapple suckers and pigeon peas were planted along the rows near the fruit trees. Forest tree species were planted around the demonstration plot to serve as a perimeter fence. With the contour line plantings serving as hedgerows, a variety of important home-use and commercial plants such as ginger, *gabi*, and banana were planted between the rows. The perennials were planted along the contour lines and the forest trees at the edges of the plot because of their ability to hold the soil and prevent erosion. Plants like pigeon peas were planted because they improve soil quality and serve as nitrogen-fixing agents.

Except for a few problems, the demonstration farms matured as scheduled. The farm in Dampig was initially destroyed by stray animals, especially goats, but through community pressure on farmers to control their animals and with hard work, the demonstration farm has recovered. There have been no technical problems in Subec although in Saliksik, coffee, which was planted between the hedgerows, is showing a relatively high mortality rate. As a means to further involve farmers in saving their environment and as an education tool, especially for farmers who are not Good Roots participants, the demonstration farms have met with considerable success. Many Good Roots farmers are taking what they have learned from the demonstration activities and applying it to their own sloping-hill farms. This is a major goal of any agricultural and community development project. Numerous government and nongovernment specialist in community development have visit the demonstration farms and asked for details on how the Good Roots systems might be replicated.

Rural Filipinos take pride in the appearance of their communities so as an environmental enhancement and beautification project, the

Good Roots staff worked with the Good Roots Associations in the *barangay* of Dampig, Subec, and San Isidro to establish road-side tree plantings. This activity was not promoted in Saliksik because there are no roads in the community. In 1992, 1,375 eucalyptus seedlings were planted by the farmers of Dampig, Subec, and San Isidro along the *barangay* roads. Unfortunately, however, a large number of the seedlings were destroyed by goats, carabao and cattle or stressed because of a lack of rainfall. There were even examples of community members cutting down the seedlings. The staff decided that roadside plantings would have greater success if the project became a community project rather than a Good Roots participant project. The Good Roots Associations joined forces with the *barangay* councils and in celebration of Fil-American Friendship Day and Philippine Independence Day in 1993 and 1994, the dead eucalyptus seedlings were replaced and the species of mahogany, suit, and *Acacia auriculiformis* were added to the roadside plantings.

Within two years, the eucalyptus of the 1992 roadside planting were more than ten meters tall. There is a freshness of air and beauty that did not exist only a few years earlier in the three communities. Because the roadside plantings in 1993 and 1994 were done by the whole community, people tend to look after the seedlings. An added benefit to the cooperative effort between the Good Roots Associations and the *barangay* council is that numerous families have become new Good Roots participants.

Because of some serious erosion problems above the village of San Isidro, the Good Roots team has worked with the *barangay* council and the Good Roots Association to establish a community wood lot. Working in association with the DENR, a 3-hectare area was identified in the forest zone of San Isidro for wood-lot production. Good Roots provided a total of 862 mahogany seedlings for planting to this area. Because of concerns with developing their watershed, the Dampig *barangay* council recently asked Good Roots for advice on how to improve the environment of their community. The Good Roots team surveyed the area and gave Dampig 302 tanguile and mahogany seedlings for planting. Good Roots continues to explore with *barangay* councils, Good Roots Associations, and other concerned citizens new ways to stabilize and restore the forest environment of the area.

Because of the Good Roots belief that children must be encouraged not to make the same environmental mistakes as their parents, considerable emphasis is placed on working with the elementary schools in the area by contributing seedlings for school projects. The work of the

San Isidro elementary school is an excellent example of how cooperation in environmental matters can be beneficial to all concerned. The Parent Teachers Association of the elementary school in San Isidro joined with Good Roots to establish a model farm on the one-half hectare back lot of the school. The Good Roots staff prepared a plan with students and parents integrating numerous species of trees and other plants. Good Roots supplied seedlings and fertilizers and under the watchful eyes of the Good Roots team, the students prepared the land and planted the seedlings. The students learned new techniques in environmental reclamation and the Good Roots staff learned about the concerns of students and their parents. Good Roots and the San Isidro PTA are especially proud of these students because they were awarded the "Best" at the provincial level in the Clean and Green program of the Philippine Department of Education, Culture and Sports.

Good Roots is constantly striving to train participants in technologies that require little or no financial expense on the part of farmers. For example, in early 1994, the Good Roots participants joined the staff at the project office in Pagudpud to learn the latest in bud-grafting techniques for mango and citrus. Grafting and budding procedures are important for the farmers to learn because enables fruit bearing trees to produce fruit in almost half the time as seedlings grown from seeds. Farmers are obviously interested in learning techniques that will lead to more immediate profitability for their efforts. The one-day course was given by the Good Roots staff and by personnel from the Twin Rivers Citrus Farm in Aparri and from the Forestry Development Project in Ilocos Norte.

At the end of the course, each participant returned home with his or her output of grafted mango and citrus seedlings for planting.

Two months after the grafting and budding course, the Good Roots team inspected the planted seedlings and found the mortality rate to be higher than expected. Neither Good Roots nor the farmers wanted to abandon the project so a follow-up training session was held for the farmers. This time, however, the training sessions were held in the Good Roots villages. Good Roots hired a retired plant propagator from the Bureau of Plant Industry in Kalinga Apayao who simplified the grafting and budding process and spent more time working one on one with the farmers. Once again, the participants carried their output of grafted and budded plants home and planted them. A follow-up by the Good Roots staff revealed that plant mortality was well within expectation. The Good Roots farmers once again have shown that environmental reclamation can come to fruition with the right attitude and through hard work.

Reclaiming ancestral lands

The activities of Good Roots has extended so far as to help people reclaim lost lands. Early in the project, the Good Roots team recognized that the Yapayao of Saliksik were farming land that technically did not belong to them. The Yapayao recognized this situation but believed that they were caught in what seemed to them an inequitable situation; they were farming land that had belonged to their ancestors but in terms of Philippine law, they were effectively squatters. The Good Roots research team brought this situation to the attention of the DENR and volunteered to survey the area in question to determine if it were possible for some of the Yapayao to qualify for a Certificate of Stewardship Contract. This legally binding contract gives the holder of the stewardship certificate the right to farm a specified piece of land for twenty-five years, renewable for another twenty-five years. Correcting a wrong of many years became a reality through the efforts of Good Roots with the cooperation of the DENR. Secretary Angel C. Alcala signed documents in December 1992 granting a Certificate of Stewardship Contract to twenty-nine Yapayao families covering an area of 55 hectares. For Good Roots then, community development is more than just plants and man.

Awards and motivation

Even with the finest technical knowledge and the extension activities of Good Roots, the project would have failed without the cooperation and hard work of the farmers. And, in Good Roots, as in any rural development project, some farmers may occasionally lose their enthusiasm and interest, or get too busy to work on the project. Realizing this possibility, Good Roots has always worked had to develop motivation techniques that will keep the participants excited about their activities.

As noted, farm families have always been involved in Good Roots decision-making—whether it be as to which site should be chosen for the nursery or which species of trees to propagate for immediate economic or environmental benefit. To insure that the project continues to generate enthusiasm for the farmers, the two major motivating activities promoted by Good Roots are educational field trips and an annual awards ceremony. Both programs have fostered goodwill and helped the participants maintain their interest.

As part of its overall program, Good Roots attempts to take farm families on at least two educational trips each year. The purpose of the trips is twofold: the education of farmers on new technologies, and to keep farmers interested in Good Roots. For example, one year the educational fieldtrip involved two busloads of participants visiting a small citrus farm and a large citrus farm in nearby provinces. Six months in advance of the trip, participants were told that only those families who actively worked in the nurseries could be accommodated on the two buses as space would be limited. The trip enabled the farmers to listen to lectures by specialists on citrus growing and see for themselves the economic potentials of citrus farming. The participants were particularly interested in the rewards and risks of budding technology and of small-farm management. Some of the participants on this trip were so enthralled with budding and grafting that they purchased budded seedlings to take back to their own farms. This enthusiasm eventually led to Good Roots seeking out a specialist in budding and grafting to conduct a seminar for the farmers.

A side benefit of these educational trips is the opportunity for Good Roots farmers from different villages to interact and discuss their successes and failures.

Good Roots participants take considerable pride in their accomplishments and in the fact that they are working together to reclaim their environment. To foster this pride, Good Roots instituted an annual awards ceremony to honor the participants.

A week or so before the day of the ceremony, the Good Roots team surveys individual family farm lots, community nurseries, and the general environmental conditions of each Good Roots *barangay*. The team carefully records the diversity and overall growth of plants, evaluates soil erosion techniques, and notes the efficiency of farm space utilization. The team pays particular attention to plant mortality rates and their care and maintenance. The findings are tabulated and the team meets formally to decide on the winners.

The Good Roots awards are: Most Active Participants (three per *barangay*); Best Good Roots Association (one for total project); Best Good Roots Association (one for total project); Best Nursery; and Most Active Association Leader (one for total project). There are also a number of lesser awards.

Over the years of Good Roots, awards day has developed into a major yearly event. Refreshments are served and speeches are made, all designed to honor the Good Roots participants for their work and success. Prizes are never in cash. Instead, the winners receive spades, spading forks, scythes, pick mattocks, hand trowels, pruning shears, rakes, wheel barrels, other farming implements, all tied and bundled with brightly colored ribbons. No participant leaves the award ceremony empty-handed. Everyone present receives at least a Good Roots T-shirt and a certificate for their involvement in Good Roots.

One of the greatest rewards for the Good Roots team, however, comes from knowing that the participants are trying to improve their lives and the health of their environment. In 1994, one participant was overheard saying to another participant: "If we work just a little harder next year, we can win the Best Model Farm Award."

7 Conclusions and postscript

Conclusions

By any measure of agroforestry and livelihood research and development, the Good Roots project is a success. At a reasonable cost and with a minimum of employees, Good Roots has helped farmers take control of their own future and put right some of their mistakes of the past. Over the many years of Good Roots, numerous independent journalists visited the Good Roots villages and reported their findings to the public. A few comments from the Good Roots participants in Pagudpud will suffice to illustrate the general attitude of the farmers as reported by journalists and translated into English (see Wallace 2001).

> I've lived in Dampig all my life. Today, even all of my children are members of Good Roots. We help plant, share information and give seedlings to other barangays, to farmers who weren't Good Roots participants. Good Roots has helped us a lot. If they see a market for our products, they also tell us. Good Roots taught us how to have a better ginger harvest and now we have bumper crops.
>
> (Florencio Viernes, Good Roots
> Association President for
> Dampig, 1991)

> We have one of the furthest barangays here. If any one needs help in planting, those of us who were with Good Roots Association help everyone. I was a farmer participant and I learned to plant a variety of plants from Good Roots. We have discovered that when people plant for themselves, they learn to appreciate their plants more. The government sometimes pays farmers to plant as a form

of assistance but Good Roots showed us a better way to motivate farmers.

(Gumercindo Balalio, Barangay Captain, 1994)

When I was in San Isidro, Good Roots gave seedlings for the schoolyard the Parent–Teacher Community Association. The school children enjoyed planting and caring for the trees and plants. In Lanao, I replicated my experience in San Isidro and it turned out even better, except I had to buy the seedlings myself. We have since cleared the two hills at the back and turned one into a mango plantation. The other hill has narra, avocado, santol, jackfruit and other fruits. We even have a waste segregation and integration facility. The alumni have been donating to the beautification of these hills but at the root of it all, of course, is all that I learned from Good Roots.

(Lilian Geologo, Principal, Lanao Elementary School, 1996)

Before Good Roots came, I planted mostly pineapple and vegetables. Today, I have camote, sitaw and more vegetables for which people nearby come to buy. Good Roots has helped me increase my income as a vendor. I used to sell only bananas in the school. I only plant around my house but Good Roots has taught me how to make better use of the land by choosing what and how to plant. I have been selling my calamansi from the seedling we raised in the nursery. It yields twice in a year. I now share my Good Roots lessons with my neighbors.

(Mila Andres, Housewife, 1995)

I now grow mahogany, mango, lemon and citrus trees on lots totaling one hectare and I am beginning to plant on a four-hectare farm. After Good Roots left, we still worked. I started to share with my fellow cooperative members all that I have learned. I am now coordinating with a representative of PHILFOODEX, a group of leading Filipino exporters as to the possibility of pooling the efforts of several barangay here so we can deliver at least ten tons of a product directly to Manila clients and eliminate middlemen.

(Cristino Claro, Good Roots Association
President for Subec, 1996)

The Good Roots Project could not have attained its high level of success unless the key components of the project—industry, government, the scientific and extension staff, and local farm families—were able to cooperate and reinforce the objectives of one another.

As noted earlier, the Good Roots Project was originally conceived as a joint effort between industry, the scientific academy, and local farm communities.

When Good Roots was initiated, the sponsor from industry was a petroleum company, Caltex (Philippines) Inc., now a part of ChevronTexaco Corporation. At no point did Caltex ever attempt to apply pressure or influence on any member of the Good Roots staff in order to skew information or research in its direction. They provided the funds for Good Roots and never asked for anything in return. The question becomes then, how does an oil company such as Caltex benefit from funding an agroforestry and livelihood research and development project? The answer is simple: it gives the company an opportunity to show the public that it wants to be a socially responsible corporation. The only thing Caltex ever asked of the Director of the project was to make an occasional media appearance or to meet with journalists. Many multinational corporations have divisions that work to improve the corporate image by supporting and working with non-profit organizations.

The Philippine DENR was the government entity sponsoring the Good Roots Project. The DENR benefited from Good Roots because it provided the government an opportunity to increase its list of successful environmental projects at no cost to itself. The project benefited from the technical support provided by the DENR. For providing technical support to the project, certain government personnel received a modest honorarium.

The enthusiasm of the Good Roots staff was maintained by providing good working conditions. This was important because the staff often worked more than twelve hours a day, seven days a week, and lived in housing similar to the families with whom they were working. The staff received a salary slightly higher than their counterparts working in government. Because they had to live away from their homes and families, they did not go home on the weekend, but instead, received a month's leave. During some slower work periods, the spouses and children of the staff were encouraged to visit them in the field. Because the project was interdisciplinary in form, and multipurpose in function, the staff agreed there were always new challenges to face, and new things to learn. This kept their job exciting. Most importantly for the staff, was the reward of knowing they were doing something that was good for their country and for the farm families with whom they were working.

After a self-evaluation of the Good Roots Project by the staff during the fifth year, it was concluded that ethnicity—Ilocano or

Yapayao—was not a major contributor to success and cooperation or to any lack of success. What might appear to be factors of ethnicity were more likely factors of history and circumstance. As in any development project, some people are more cooperative than others, some individuals more hard working than others, and some more resistant to change than others. In general, most of the Ilocano families and Yapayao families in the project were cooperative and supportive of Good Roots. There was only one instance during the five years of Good Roots in Pagudpud that a group of participants had to be chastised for their failure to uphold their part of the bargain they made with Good Roots. In this case, a simple reminder that many more families wanted to work with Good Roots than the staff could possibly accommodate was sufficient to correct the situation.

Neither sex nor age were critical variables accounting for success or failure in Good Roots. There were males with newly formed families that were active participants in Good Roots just as there were old men and women who were active participants. As is the agricultural norm among the Ilocano and the Yapayao, the men tended to do more of the heavy-duty work associated with nursery construction and maintenance, and the women tended to do more of the potting activities. When it came to grafting and budding, the women became the more skilled workers.

If age, sex, and culture does not account for variations in success (as there were no outright failures) within communities of Good Roots, what then might account for these differences? Fundamentally, five factors conditioned the degree to which certain families and communities excelled in Good Roots. These are: (1) leadership; (2) economic status; (3) association with government projects; (4) location; and (5) relationship with the Good Roots staff.

A significant factor contributing to the success or a lack of it in the Good Roots Project was community leadership. Among the Ilocano, a willingness to take on the difficult job, and work long and hard, commands respect. Respect is earned through hard work. Success came easier to those Good Roots communities where leadership was strong, regardless of leader gender and whether such leadership was provided singly or in a group. If there were two or more males and female leaders, successes came even easier. This kind of leadership wielded more power and was more influential than that coming from an elected *barangay* captain. A strong and supportive *barangay* captain can be a great help to Good Roots. But, a weak or uncooperative *barangay* captain generally created few problems for Good Roots provided the leadership of the Good Roots Association was strong.

Among the Yapayao, the men who contributed most to the success of Good Roots were hard workers who had already established themselves as leaders in the community through traditional cultural means, and through their involvement in a rebellious and illegal political group. Yapayao women actively participated in the Good Roots Project, but their role was as followers rather than leaders.

Although the economic status of the Ilocano Good Roots participant families represented a typical cross-section for Northern Luzon, the poorer families were the most eager of the economic groups to join Good Roots. All economic groups embraced Good Roots, but the poorer families clearly saw the project as an opportunity to improve their livelihood. These families had the most to gain. The Good Roots staff emphasized livelihood with these participants. With the small landholding families or financially more secure families, the Good Roots staff emphasized both environmental reclamation and livelihood. Although the few wealthy families in the Pagudpud area and absentee landlords, did not oppose Good Roots, they were generally neutral on the project.

Since the Yapayao were generally the poorest of the poor, the focus was on livelihood activities.

The Good Roots staff learned early in the project that the Ilocano farmers of the Pagudpud area had been exposed to a several government development projects. They also learned quickly that the farmers in the government projects were used to being paid for participating. Paying farmers to improve their own environment and livelihood was contrary to the Good Roots philosophy. Consequently, a major hurdle that the Good Roots staff had to overcome was to persuade farm families that their efforts would be rewarded at a later date. Those families that had never participated in government projects tended to join Good Roots more quickly than those farmers who had earlier been paid by the government.

The Yapayao families had never worked on government projects. The more remote the location of the farm families, the more enthusiasm they tended to show for the Good Roots Project, that is, they were the most easy to recruit. A part of this was tied directly to economic status in that the poorer families tended to be the most geographically isolated families. Another part of it was these families had never been asked to participate in any kind of development project.

Although the factors of leadership, economic status, location, and participation in government projects are important variables conditioning the degree to which farm families actively participated in Good Roots, the factor that stands out most noticeably is the degree to which the Good Roots staff was able to establish rapport in the community. Unfortunately, the conclusions on this matter are impressionistic. It is clear, however, that when rapport was relatively easy to establish, the chances for Good Roots being successful greatly improved. In fact, in the few communities where the research team encountered resistance or found a lack of interest, the team may have been better off to have abandoned their goal and move on to another community.

Postscript

By the fourth year of the research and development activities in Pagudpud, all the evidence suggested that the project had reached a high level of sustainability, and that the participants were sufficiently trained and committed to carry on without the direct help of the Good Roots staff. The Good Roots team had effectively worked themselves out of a job, the highest compliment that could be given to them by the people of Pagudpud. The major question then became: where else in the Philippines could the lessons learned in Pagudpud be best applied.

Many areas were considered and visited—from small islands to the mountains of the Cordillera Central. It was finally decided that Good Roots could make the greatest contribution to the environment, and to the Filipino people by selecting a rural area that was both similar to, but also markedly different from Pagudpud. It was decided that the project should be moved to an area that was more densely populated, and which had a different historical and cultural background. This would allow the Good Roots team to apply the theories and methods developed in Pagudpud to a different situation, and make sure the successes of Pagudpud were not culturally based or unique to that environment. Good Roots moved to the community of Lobo, Batangas, in January 1977.

The municipality of Lobo, a southern Tagalog-speaking community of 37,000 people, is located at the end of a gravel and partially paved road that winds through mountainous terrain some 36 kilometers from Batangas City, and 148 kilometers south of Manila. Except for the *poblacion* and some coastal areas, the community is characterized by a hilly to mountainous topography. The two highest mountain peaks are Mt Banoy and Mt Naguiling, both of which still house small pockets of primary forest. Almost half of the eastern part of Lobo is cut off from the rest of the community during the rainy season because of a river that regularly floods the area.

The Good Roots team learned during the survey of the Lobo region that three socio-economic practices characterizing Pagudpud were not a feature of Lobo: charcoal-making from trees, cutting trees for fuel-wood, and illegal logging. These activities were insignificant in Lobo. Because Lobo is a large copra production area, there is an abundance of coconut shells in the area. So, instead of making charcoal from cut trees, the people make charcoal from coconut shells, thus effectively using the resources of the environment. In addition, because Lobo is more prosperous than Pagudpud, more of the farm families can afford to use propane gas. It is also more readily available. There was no need for the Good Roots team to work with the farmers to develop fast-growing tree species to be used for fuelwood. Except on some remote mountains, and only at the highest elevation, there is no primary forest in Lobo. Most of the land was logged over and converted to coconut plantations during the last century. Consequently, illegal logging is of little importance in Lobo. With the absence of these three environmental factors in Lobo, the Good Roots team could devote their efforts exclusively to helping the farmers stabilize a degenerating environment through forestry activities, and improve their livelihood with the introduction of modern upland agricultural methods.

One, of many, lessons learned in Pagudpud was that while rural Filipinos are willing to share in the reward of establishing communal nurseries, fundamentally, they prefer to maintain their own household nursery. The plan for Good Roots Lobo was first to establish communal nurseries in selected *barangay*, and then slowly close down these nurseries in favor of household nurseries. This transition was accomplished by the third year of the project.

By the fourth year of Good Roots, in Lobo, it was clear that farm families of Lobo were not only able, but also willing, to assume responsibility for the Good Roots Project. The Good Roots goals in Lobo had come easier and faster in Lobo than in Pagudpud, primarily because of the experience of the Good Roots team, and the opportunity to limit the focus of the development activities to hard wood tree species, fruit tree species, and the introduction of modern upland farming techniques. At the annual award ceremony in the year 2000, the Good Roots Project was formally turned over to the community of Lobo.

The following year, the Good Roots Project moved to the community of Pugo, in the province of La Union, located 250 kilometers north of Manila. A major purpose of this move was to test the multipurpose research and development approaches employed in Pagudpud and Lobo in another environment and under different conditions. Pugo is a markedly different community from Pagudpud and Lobo. It is located along a heavily traveled highway leading to one of the major cities in the Philippines. This city, Baguio, is often referred to as the "summer capital" of the country, and known for its vegetables. Pugo is only 40 kilometers from Baguio, and although rural, is far more urban in orientation than Pagudpud and Lobo, is more cash dependant, and reflects the cultural homogenization of a rapidly modernizing Philippines. Because of these factors, the challenges for Good Roots are significantly different from those faced in Pagudpud and Lobo. Responding to the needs and wishes of the farmers of Pugo, Good Roots is focusing on fruit tree species, modern farming on small plots of land, and general community development. If the lessons learned in Pagudpud and Lobo are applied judiciously, there is no reason to doubt the outcome of Good Roots, Pugo.

It is anticipated that after over a decade of research and development, the plants of Good Roots will stand through time as a tribute to numerous men and women who believe in two simple but compelling ideas: that rural environmental reclamation and economic development may be effectively implemented with dramatic results by helping farmers help themselves, and by encouraging farm families to place their future in their own hands. The many years of Good Roots reflect the dedication, labor, and aspirations of many people—farmers, scientists, business people, and politicians, all believing in these ideas and ideals.

Glossary

abirat	Kin term: the spouse of Ego's *gayam* (Yapayao)
abokado	Avocado (Filipino)
abuyon	Reciprocal labor arrangement (Yapayao)
adaan	*Albizia procera* (Ilocano)
ading	Younger male or female (Ilocano)
agandong	*Trema orientalis* (Ilocano)
agasaksak	Thrashing the grain (Ilocano)
agbila/agbilag	Drying the *palay* (Yapayao)
agdan	Ladder to a house (Ilocano)
agirik	Thrashing the grain (Ilocano)
agkakabbalay	Household (Ilocano)
agkokobon	Household (Yapayao)
aglipayano	A follower of the *Iglesia Filipina Independiente* religion
agpungo	Bundling the reserve rice seed (Yapayao)
agraras/maguma	Cutting small vegetation in the *uma* (Yapayao)
agraw	*Premna odorateblanco* (Ilocano)
agsaksi	Going to municipal hall to obtain marriage license (Ilocano)
alem	*Mallotus multiglandulosus* (Ilocano)
algarrobo	Rain Tree (Filipino)
algarrobo	*Samanea saman* (Ilocano)
alinao	*Grewia multiflora* (Ilocano)
aliwa	Head axe (Yapayao)
allokon	*Broussonetia luzunica* (Ilocano)

aludig	*Streblus asper* (Ilocano)
alumamani	*Pittosporum pentandrum* (Ilocano)
alupa	*Lapptea* spp. (Ilocano)
alupat nuang	*Dendrocnicle meyeniana* (Ilocano)
ama	Kin term: Ego's father (Yapayao)
amamali	*Leea aculata* (Ilocano)
ammuyo/abuyog/inkaruan	Reciprocal labor arrangement (Yapayao)
amugis	*Koordersiodendro pinnatum* (Ilocano)
anahaw	A palm used in thatching, weaving, construction
anak	Kin term: Ego's male or female child (Ilocano)
anak	Kin term: Ego's children and children of his or her brothers and sisters (Yapayao)
anangka	Jackfruit (Ilocano)
anangka	*Artocarpus heterophyllus* (Ilocano)
an-anib	Amulet (Ilocano and Yapayao)
anito	Amorphous spirit (Ilocano)
anito	A ritual to drive away spirits and cure illness (Yapayao)
anonang	*Anona reticulata* (Ilocano)
anteng	*Toona asperum* (Ilocano)
anubing	*Artocarpus ovatus* (Iloccano)
apatot	*Morinda bracteata* (Ilocano)
apitong	*Dipterocarpus grandiflorus* (Ilocano)
aplas	*Ficus congesta* (Ilocano)
aplis	*Ficus ulmifolia* (Ilocano)
apnit	*Shorea contorta* (Ilocano)
apo	Kin term: Ego's children's children (Ilocano)
apo	Kin term: Ego's father's mother and mother's mother (Yapayao)
apoko	Kin term: Ego's children's children (Ilocano)
apoko ti tumeng	Kin term: Ego's children's children's children (Ilocano)
apo na buwal	Kin term: females of Ego's third ascending generation (Yapayao)

apug	Lime (Yapayao)
arupagan	Apprentice Yapayao medium/healer
arusip	*Symplocos ahernii* (Ilocano)
asawa	Kin term: spouse (Ilocano, Yapayao)
asawang	Evil spirit creatures who wanders about during the night (Ilocano)
asawang	half human and half black crow creature (Yapayao)
atis	Sugar Apple (Filipino)
atong	A fire that burns in front of the house of a deceased person (Ilocano)
auri	Acacia (Filipino)
avocado	*Persea gratissima* (Ilocano)
awan a badbadjong ko	"I have no dress." (Ilocano)
baag	G-string (Yapayao)
*baake*n	*Chrisocheton pentandrus* (Ilocano)
baar	Two tied *pungo* (Yapayao)
baggoong	Filipino fish sauce
bago	*Macaranga bicolor* (Ilocano)
bagobo	Pili Nut (Ilocano)
bahala na	Fatalism (Filipino)
balinghasai	*Buchanania arborescens* (Ilocano)
ballas	A small hoe (Yapayao)
ballawa	House for storing human skulls (Yapayao)
banger	*Sterculia foetida* (Ilocano)
bangles	*Palaquium philippense* (Ilocano)
barabad	White headband worn during mourning (Ilocano)
barangay	Filipino equivalent of village
bari-bari	a request for safe passage from spirits (Ilocano)
barong tagalog	Elegant Filipino man's shirt worn on formal occasions
baroy	*Pterospermum cebicum* (Ilocano)
basar-basar	*Ficus pseodopalma* (Ilocano)
basi	Filipino native rice wine
*bayaba*s	*Psidium gaujava* (Ilocano)
beriba	*Rollinia mucosa* (Ilocano)
binai pugo	*Antisdesma penfandrum* (Ilocano)

binggas	*Terminalia citrine* (Ilocano)
biraw	The ritual sharing and chewing of betel nut (Yapayao)
biruka	Another term of *asawang* (Yapayao)
bitaog	*Callophyllum inophyllum* (Ilocano)
bitor	Formal giving of gifts ritual for newly married couple (Ilocano)
bolo	Term for machete used on Northern Luzon
bua	Betel nut (Ilocano and Yapayao)
bugnay	*Antisdesma bunius* (Ilocano)
bulala	*Naucle orientalis* (Ilocano)
butnong	*Kleinhovia hospita* (Ilocano)
carabao	Filipino terms for water buffalo
cayo-cayo	A shout asking malevolent spirits to leave the vicinity (Ilocano)
cogon	A tenacious grass
dalagan	Inclined bed
dalipaweng	*Alstonia scholaris* (Ilocano)
dalunot	*Pipturus arborescens* (Ilocano)
damortis	*Pitchecellobium dulce* (Ilocano)
dangla	*Vitex negundo* (Ilocano)
danupra	*Toona sureni* (Ilocano)
dayo-dayo	A shout used to frighten away malevolent creatures (Ilocano)
digos nga ruot	Herbal water for cleansing people contaminated by malevolent spirits (Yapayao)
dogmon	Pomelo (Ilocano)
dugmon	*Citrus grandis* (Ilocano)
dungon	Narra (Filipino)
dungon	*Pterocarpus indicus* (Ilocano)
durrarakit	Yapayao medium/healer
durrarakit na mangngagas	A senior Yapayao medium/healer
duweg	*Bischofia javanica* (Ilocano)
ebbal	Edema
gaddang	A dibble for planting (Yapayao)
gasat	Birth fate (Ilocano)
gayam	Kin term: Ego's siblings (Yapayao)
gayobano	Soursop (Filipino)
gisi	Tattoo (Yapayao)
grandilla	Passion Fruit (Ilocano)

guapol	Guava (Ilocano)
herbolaryo	Traditional medical practitioner (Ilocano)
hilot	Traditional Filipino birth attendant
igio	*Dysoxylum arborescens* (Ilocano)
Iglesia Filipina Independiente	A religious institution founded in 1898
Iglesia ni Kristo	A Filipino religious movement founded in 1914
ikit	Kin term: Ego's father's or mother's sister (Ilocano)
ina	Kin term: Ego's mother (Yapayao)
inang	Kin term: mother of Ego (Ilocano)
inapugan	Yapayao wedding ceremony
inkaruan	Reciprocal labor arrangement (Yapayao)
ipag	Kin term: Ego's spouse's sister (Ilocano)
ipil	*Intsia bijuga* (Ilocano)
kaannakan	Children of Ego's brothers and sisters
kabagyan	Relatives (Ilocano)
kabagyan	Consanguineal or affinal relative (Yapayao)
kabsat a babai	Kin term: Ego's sister (Ilocano)
kabsat a lalaki	Kin term: Ego's brother (Ilocano)
kaburaw	*Citrus grandis* (Ilocano)
kadir	*Duabanga moluccana* (Ilocano)
kahel	Pink Pomelo (Ilocano)
kaibaan	Spirits that appear as beautiful young men or women covered with numerous tattoos (Yapayao)
kaingin	Filipino term for slash-and-burn farming
kakaw	Cacao (Ilocano)
kakay	Kin term: Ego's father's father and mother's father (Yapayao)
kakay na buwal	Kin term: males of Ego's third ascending generation (Yapayao)
kalamamsi	Calamansi (Filipino)
kalolot	*Artocarpus rubrovenius* (Ilocano)
kalubkob	*Syzgium calubcob* (Ilocano)

kalupit	*Terminalia microcarpa* (Ilocano)
kamatis	Tomato (Filipino)
kamiring	*Semecarpus philippinensis* (Ilocano)
kapas	Kapok (Ilocano)
kape	Philippine Coffee (Ilocano)
kapiddua	Kin term: Ego's second degree cousin (Ilocano)
kapidua	Kin term: Ego's second degree cousins (Yapayao)
kapinsan	Kin term: Ego's fathers' and mother's brothers and sisters (Yapayao)
karabasa	Squash (Filipino)
kardis	Pigeon Pea (Ilocano)
karmay	Star Fruit (Ilocano)
kasinsin	Kin term: Ego's brother's or sister's children (Ilocano)
kasoy	Cashew Nut ((Ilocano)
katugangan	Kin term: father and mother of Ego's spouse (Ilocano)
katugangan	Kin term: Ego's wife's father and mother (Yapayao)
katugangan a babai	Ego's mother-in-law
katugangan a lalaki	Ego's father-in-law
kayong	Kin term: Spouse's brother (Ilocano)
kayong	Kin term: Ego's wife's sister and brother; Ego's siblings' spouses (Yapayao)
komitis	*Leucana leococephala* (Ilocano)
komkompitis	Ipil-ipil (Ilocano)
kugit	Circumcision (Ilocano)
kumpay	Small hand knife for harvesting *palay* (Ilocano)
kusibeng	*Sapindus saponaria* (Ilocano)
labig	Anahaw (Ilocano)
labuyok	*Macranga grandifolia* (Ilocano)
lansones	Lansones (Filipino)
lanuti	*Wrightia pubescens* (Ilocano)
latabak	*Ficus variegata* (Ilocano)
lingo-lingo	*Viticipremna philippinensis* (Ilocano)

lola	Kin term: Ego's father's mother (Ilocano)
lola ti tuod	Kin term: Ego's father's father's mother (Ilocano)
lolo	Kin term: Ego's father's father (Ilocano)
lolo ti tuod	Kin term: Ego's father's father's father (Ilocano)
looc	Bay or cove (Tagalog)
lualo	Opening prayer at wedding reception (Ilocano)
lumboy	*Syzgium cumini* (Ilocano)
mabalsan	Possessed by a spirit (Yapayao)
madre	*Gliricidia sepium* (Ilocano)
magakkat	Re-burning the *kaingin* (Yapayao)
magallap	Harvesting taro, harvesting the *palay* (Yapayao)
magballa	Weeding the *uma* (Yapayao)
magbalolas ku gabit	Weeding between the taro (Yapayao)
magbanti/mamugaw	Protecting the *kaingin* (Yapayao)
magkallang	Cutting large trees in the *uma* (Yapayao)
magkuman ku gabit	Planting taro (Yapayao)
maglugam	Clearing the *uma* for vegetables (Yapayao)
maglugam/magballas	Re-weeding the *uma* (Yapayao)
magmula	Planting vegetables (Yapayao)
magrangas	Cutting felled trees in the *uma* (Yapayao)
magtabno	Planting rice in the *kaingin* (Yapayao)
mahogani	Big leaf mahogany (Filipino)
makabulan	Feast one month after death (Ilocano)
makadeg	*Dracontomelon dao* (Ilocano)
makasiyam	Feast nine days after death (Ilocano)
makatawen	Year anniversary feast after death
malay-laya	Selecting the *uma* site (Yapayao)
maliket	Small bundle of upland ritual rice (Yapayao)

malugai	*Pometia pinnata* (Ilocano)
mamaen	Mixture of betel nut, lime, and water (Yapayao)
mammullo	Medical specialist in mending bones, muscles, joints, etc. (Ilocano)
manaligat	Preparing to harvest the *palay* (Yapayao)
manaltalon/magabalasibas	Marking the *uma* site (Yapayao)
manang	Older female (Ilocano)
mandarin	Mandarin Orange (Filipino)
manding	Antique Chinese bead (Yapayao)
mangablon	Traditional midwife (Ilocano)
mangga	Mango (Ilocano)
mangipenpen	Storing the *palay* (Yapayao)
mannamay	Witch (Ilocano)
mannuma	A medical specialist in sucking venom from poisonous bites (Ilocano)
manong	Older male (Ilocano)
manugang	Kin term: sons and daughters of Ego's sisters and brothers (Ilocano)
manugang	Kin term: children of Ego's brothers and sisters (Yapayao)
marapapaya	*Polyscias nodosa* (Ilocano)
mara sablot	*Pinturus arborescens* (Ilocano)
maratabako	*Elephantopus tomentosus* (Ilocano)
maratebbeg	*Ficus congesta* (Ilocano)
maratekka	*Albizia saponaria* (Ilocano)
mariapa	Old Chinese jar (Yapayao)
mayapis	*Shorea squamata* (Ilocano)
minatay a nabaybay-an	Spirits of bodies buried and abandoned under the house (Yapayao)
ninang	Sponsor or godmother (Ilocano)
ninong	Sponsor or godfather (Ilocano)
niog	Coconut (Ilocano)
obien	*Artocarpus rubrovenius* (Ilocano)
pagagapas	Harvesting the paddy (Ilocano)
paguringun	*Cratoxylum sumatranum* (Ilocano)
paitan	*Cleidion javanicum* (Ilocano)
pakak	Breadfruit (Ilocano)
pakak baker	*Artocarpus blancoi* (Ilocano)

palali	*Dillenia philippinesis* (Ilocano)
palay	Rice during growth and at harvested
pamittaogen	*Callophyllum blancoi* (Ilocano)
panagabuno	Paddy maintenance (Ilocano)
panagarado	First plowing (Ilocano)
panagaramid iti pagbunobonan	Preparing rice seed beds (Ilocano)
panagbilag iti irik	Drying the *palay* (Ilocano)
panagbugaw	Protecting the paddy (Ilocano)
panagbunobon	Sowing seeds (Ilocano)
panaggaikpanagparagus	Weeding the paddy (Ilocano)
panagidulin	Storing the *palay* (Ilocano)
panagkiwar	Final plowing (Ilocano)
panagmoriski	Harrowing (Ilocano)
panagpaati	Draining the paddy (Ilocano)
panagpabayo	Milling the *palay* (Ilocano)
panagpadanum	Irrigating the field (Ilocano)
panagudno	Asking permission of a girl's parents to plan a wedding (Ilocano)
panganuladsien	*Alstonia macrophylla* (Ilocano)
panglakayen	A spokesman representing a girl's parents preparing for marriage (Ilocano)
pangleongboyen	*Syzytium simile* (Ilocano)
panua wen	A judicial council composed of older and respected men (Yapayao)
pao	*Mangifera altisima* (Ilocano)
papaya	Papaya (Filipino)
partera	Midwife (Spanish)
parya	Bittergourd (Ilocano)
patangis	*Talauma villeriana* (Ilocano)
patong	A class of Yapayao rituals
patong a parangpang	Initiation feast of a neophyte understudy into the world of the medium (Yapayao)
patong a parubuat	A feast held when an important leader, medium, or politician dies (Yapayao)
patong a saong	Ancestor feast designed to dissuade spirits of the dead from entering the world of the living (Yapayao)

patong a sinang-at	A curing feast held for a gravely ill person (Yapayao)
patong a tugot	A feast associated with a marriage (Yapayao)
pildes	*Garcinia dives* (Ilocano)
pinya	Pineapple (Filipino)
pisek	*Shorea guiso* (Ilocano)
pitobulan	Feast seven months after death (Ilocano)
poblacion	The central area of a town
pungo	Six tied *pusot* (Yapayao)
purok	Filipino equivalent to a neighborhood
pusot	Smallest bundle of tied *palay* (Yapayao)
putik	A Chinese jar heirloom (Yapayao)
quen	Wrap-around skirt (Yapayao)
rakem	Small knife for harvesting *palay* (Yapayao)
rambutan	Rambutan (Filipino)
rayya-rayya	*Ficus septica* (Ilocano)
sablot	*Litsea sebifera* (Ilocano)
sab-ong	Brideprice (Ilocano)
saget	*Vitex parviflora* (Ilocano)
Sakai ni Jehova	A Filipino non-denominational religious group
sakat	*Terminalia nitens* (Ilocano)
salamagi	Tamerind (Ilocano)
salbang	*Erythrima orientalis* (Ilocano)
samak	*Macaranga tanarius* (Ilocano)
santol	Santol (Filipino)
sarab	A process of mat-wrapping a new mother
sarakat	Pandan (Ilocano)
sarikampo	Leader of the *panua wen* (Yapayao)
sarimbaboy	*Cratoxylum sumatranum* (Ilocano)
sari-sari	A small store selling minor foods and supplies
seggay	*Shorea astylosa* (Ilocano)
sigay	Small temporary house in *uma* (Yapayao)
sili	Sweet pepper (Ilocano)

sitaw	String bean (Ilocano)
suit	Philippine aṣh (Filipino)
sumgab	Burning the *kaingin* (Yapayao)
sungat	Individuals with hidden marks on their forehead who are dangerous to pregnant women (Ilocano)
tabau-tabua	Luffa (Ilocano)
taingang babui	*Gonocaryum calleryanum* (Ilocano)
tangili	*Shorea polysperma* (Ilocano)
tanguile	Red Luan (Filipino)
tanguili	*Shorea polysperma* (Ilocano)
tarong	Eggplant (Ilocano)
tatang	Kin term: father of ego (Ilocano)
tebbeg	*Ficus nota* (Ilocano)
tennab	A long bath alternating between hot and cold water
tombac	Retaining wall between rice paddies (Ilocano)
traja de boda	Wedding dress (Ilocano)
tunek	Start of the transplanting season (Ilocano)
tutupac	Gifts given to newly married couple (Ilocano)
uas	*Harpulia arborea* (Ilocano)
ugat ng buhay	The roots of life (Tagalog)
ules	Native woven blanket (Yapayao)
uliteg	Kin term: Ego's father's or mother's brother (Ilocano)
uma	Yapayao slash and burn plot (Yapayao)
utong na loob	A debt of the heart (Tagalog)
uyong/uyon	Ten tied *baar* (Yapayao)
yalingan	*Pterospermum diversifolium* (Ilocano)

References

Barraclough, Solon L. and Krishna B. Ghimire (2000) *Agricultural Expansion and Tropical Deforestation*, London and Sterling: Earthscan Publications Ltd.

Benner, Timothy J. (2001) "Contextual Issues in the Measurement and Definition of Poverty: Poverty in the Rural Philippines," PhD Dissertation in Anthropology, Southern Methodist University.

Beyer H. Otley (1913) *The Apayao*, Beyer Collection of Manuscripts, the Itneg-Kalinga People, Paper 75.

Brown, Katrina and David W. Pearce (eds) (1994) *The Causes of Tropical Deforestation*, Vancouver, WA: UBC Press.

CGIAR (1978) *Farming Systems Research at the International Research Centers*, Washington, DC: Consultative Group on International Agricultural Research.

De Walt, B.R. (1985) "Anthropology, Sociology, and Farming Systems Research," *Human Organization* 44: 106–114.

Eggan, Fred (1960) "The Sagada Lgorots of Northern Luzon," in G.P. Murdock (ed.), *Social Structure in Southeast Asia*, Chicago, IL: Quadrangle Books, pp. 24–50.

Faculo, A. (1935) "Wedding and Other Rites in Apayao," *Philippine Magazine* 32: 285–302.

Food and Agriculture Organization of the United Nations (FAO) (2001) *State of the World's Forests 2001*, Rome.

Food and Agriculture Organization of the United Nations (FAO) (2003a) *State of the World's Forests 2003*, Rome.

Food and Agriculture Organization of the United Nations (FAO) (2003b) "Forests and Forestry: FAO and Its Work," Rome.

Jocano, F. Landa (1982) *The Ilocanos: An Ethnography of Family and Community Life in the Ilocos Region*, Quezon City: University of Philippine Press.

Jones, Jeffry R. and Ben J. Wallace (1986) *Social Sciences and Farming Systems Research: Methodological Perspectives on Agricultural Development*, Boulder, CO and London: Westview Press.

Keesing, Felix (1962) "The Isneg: Shifting Cultivators of the Northern Philippines," *Southwestern Journal of Anthropology* 18: 1–19.

Khon Kaen University (1987) *Proceeding of the 1985 International Conference on Rapid Rural Appraisal*, Khon Kaen, Rural Systems and Research and Farming Systems Research Project.

King, Victor T. (1999) *Anthropology and Development in South-East Asia: Theory and Practice*, Kuala Lumpur: Oxford University Press.

Lee, Sun-Hee (1985) *Why People Tend to Move: Individual and Community-Level Factors of Out-Migration in the Philippines*, Boulder, CO: Westview Press.

Lewis, Henry T. (1971) *Ilocano Rice Farmers: A Comparative Study of Two Philippine Barrios*, Honolulu, HI: University of Hawaii Press.

Lewis, Henry T. (1991) *Ilocano Irrigation: The Corporate Resolution*, Honolulu, HI: University of Hawaii Press.

Miller, K. and L. Tangley (1991) *Trees of Life: Saving Tropical Forests and Their Biological Wealth*, Boston, MA: Beacon Press.

Myers, Norman (1980) *Conversion of Tropical Moist Forests*, Washington, DC: National Academy of Science.

Nadkarni, M.V. with S.A. Pasha and L.S. Prabhakar (1989) *The Political Economy of Forest Use and Management*, New Delhi: Sage Publications.

National Aeronautics and Space Administration (NASA) (1998) "Tropical Deforestation," *NASA Facts*, Goddard Space Flight Center: Maryland.

Norman, D., D.H. Gilbert, and F. Winch (1979) *Farming Systems Research for Agricultural Development*, Washington, DC: US Agency for International Development.

Raintree, J.B. and M.W. Hoskins (1988) "Appropriate Research and Development Support for Forestry Extension," in RWEDP, *Planning Forestry Extension Programmes*, Bangkok: FAO.

Raros, Romy (1987) "Agroforestry Education and Training for Rural Development," in E.A. Bernardo, S.P. Sandoval, and J.S. Tan (eds), *Training Agricultural and Rural Personnel for Agroforestry Education*, Baybay, Visayas State College of Agriculture: Leyte State University, pp. 68–70.

Rhodes, R.E., D.E. Horton, and R.H. Booth (1986) "Anthropologist, Biological Scientist and Economist: The Three Musketeers or Three Stooges of Farming Systems Research," in J.R. Jones and B.J. Wallace (eds), *Social Sciences and Farming Systems Research*, Boulder, CO and London: Westview Press.

Rutten, V.W. (1982) *Agricultural Research Policy*, Minneapolis, MN: University of Minnesota Press.

Scheans, Daniel J. (1964) "The Apayao of Ilocos Norte," *Ethnohistory* 11: 394–398.

Shaner, W.W., P.F. Philipp, and W.R. Schmehl (1982) *Farming Systems Research and Development: Guidelines for Developing Countries*, Boulder, CO: Westview Press.

Smith, Peter C. (1981) *Population Pressure and Social Response on the Ilocos Coast in the Philippines*, Honolulu, HI: The East–West Population Institute.

Sponsel, Leslie E., Thomas N. Headland, and Robert C. Bailey (eds) (1996) *Tropical Deforestation: The Human Dimension*, New York: Columbia University Press.

Uitamo, Elina (1999) "Modelling Deforestation Caused by the Expansion of Subsistence Farming in the Philippines," *Journal of Forest Economics* 5: 100–122.

Vanoverbergh, Maurice (1932) "The Isneg," *Publications of the Catholic Anthropological Conference* 3: 1–18.

Vanoverbergh, Maurice (1936) "The Isneg Life Cycle I. Birth, Education and Daily Routine," *Publications of the Catholic Anthropological Conference* 3: 81–186.

Vanoverbergh, Maurice (1938a) "Moral Code: The Isneg Life Cycle," *Publications of the Catholic Anthropological Conference* 3: 13–149.

Vanoverbergh, Maurice (1938b) "The Isneg Life Cycle II. Marriage, Death and Burial," *Publications of the Catholic Anthropological Conference* 3: 187–280.

Vanoverbergh, Maurice (1941) "The Isneg Farmer," *Publications of the Catholic Anthropological Conference* 3: 281–386.

Vanoverbergh, Maurice (1950) "The Isneg Body and Its Ailments," *Annali Lateranensi* 14: 193–293.

Vanoverbergh, Maurice (1953) "Isneg Constructions," *Philippine Journal of Science* 81: 77–107.

Vanoverbergh, Maurice (1953–1955) "Religion and Magic Among the Isneg," *Anthropos* 48: 71–104, 557–568; 49: 233–275, 1004–1012; 50: 212–240.

Von Carlowitz, P.G. (1984) "Multipurpose Trees and Shrubs: Opportunities and Limitations," The Establishment of a Multipurpose Tree Data Base, Working Paper No. 17, Nairobi, International Council for Research in Agroforestry.

Wallace, Ben J. (1989) "Multipurpose Tree Species: A Perspective on On-Farm Research Priority and Design," in S. Sukmana, P. Amir, and D.M. Mulyadi (eds), *Development in Procedures for Farming Systems Research, International Workshop, 1989*, Bogor, Indonesia.

Wallace, Ben J. (1991) "Using an Airplane for an Ox Cart: A Perspective on Interdisciplinary Research," *Reviews in Anthropology* 176: 163–172.

Wallace, Ben J. (1995a) "How Many Trees Does it Take to Cook a Pot of Rice? Fuelwood Consumption in Four Philippine Communities," *Human Organization* 54: 182–186.

Wallace, Ben J. (1995b) *Good Roots—Ugat ng buhay: Helping Farmers Reclaim Their Environment*, Manila: Caltex (Philippines) Inc.

Wallace, Ben J. (2001) *Good Roots II—Inheriting the Earth*, Manila: Caltex (Philippines) Inc.

Werndstedt, Frederick and J.E. Spencer (1967) *The Philippine Island World*, Berkeley, CA: The University of California Press.

Wilson, Laurence L. (1947) *Apayao Life and Legends*, Manila: Ateneo de Manila University Press.

Withington, D., K.G. MacDicken, K.G. Sastry, and N.R. Adams (eds) (1988) *Multipurpose Tree Species for Small-Farm Use*, Arlington, VA: Winrock International Institute for Agricultural Development.

Index